How to

In this issue

The 92 daily readings in this issue of *Explore* are designed to help you understand and apply the Bible as you read it each day.

It's serious!

We suggest that you allow 15 minutes each day to work through the Bible passage with the notes. It should be a meal, not a snack! Readings from other parts of the Bible can throw valuable light on the study passage. These cross-references can be skipped if you are already feeling full up, but will expand your grasp of the Bible. *Explore* uses the NIV2011 Bible translation, but you can also use it with the NIV1984 or ESV translations.

Sometimes a prayer box will encourage you to stop and pray through the lessons—but it is always important to allow time to pray for God's Spirit to bring his word to life, and to shape the way we think and live through it.

We're serious!

All of us who work on *Explore* share a passion for getting the Bible into people's lives. We fiercely hold to the Bible as God's word— to honour and follow, not to explain away.

1 Find a time you can read the Bible each day

2 Find a place where you can be quiet and think

3 Ask God to help you understand

4 Carefully read through the Bible passage for today

5 Study the verses with *Explore*, taking time to think

6 Pray about what you have read

thegoodbook COMPANY

Opening up the Bible

Welcome to Explore

Being a Christian isn't a skill you learn, like carpentry or flower arranging. Nor is it a lifestyle choice, like the kind of clothes you wear, or the people you choose to hang out with. It's about having a real relationship with the living God through his Son, Jesus Christ. The Bible tells us that this relationship is like a marriage.

It's important to start with this, because many Christians view the practice of daily Bible-reading as a Christian duty, or a hard discipline that is just one more thing to get done in our busy modern lives.

But the Bible is God speaking to us: opening his mind to us on how he thinks, what he wants for us and what his plans are for the world. And most importantly, it tells us what he has done for us in sending his Son, Jesus Christ, into the world. It's the way the Spirit shows Jesus to us, and changes us as we behold his glory.

The Bible is not a manual. It's a love letter. And as with any love letter, we'll want to treasure it, and make time to read and re-read it, so we know we are loved, and discover how we can please the one who loves us. Here are a few suggestions for making your daily time with God more of a joy than a burden:

- *Time:* Find a time when you will not be disturbed, and when the cobwebs are cleared from your mind. Many people have found that the morning is the best time as it sets you up for the day. If you're not a "morning person", then last thing at night or a mid-morning break might suit you. Whatever works for you is right for you.

- *Place:* Jesus says that we are not to make a great show of our religion *(see Matthew 6:5-6)*, but rather, to pray with the door to our room shut. Some people plan to get to work a few minutes earlier and get their Bible out in an office or some other quiet corner.

- *Prayer:* Although *Explore* helps with specific prayer ideas from the passage, try to develop your own lists to pray through. Use the flap inside the back cover to help with this. And allow what you read in the Scriptures to shape what you pray for yourself, the world and others.

- *Share:* As the saying goes, *expression deepens impression.* So try to cultivate the habit of sharing with others what you have learned. Why not join our Facebook group to share your encouragements, questions and prayer requests? Search for *Explore: For your daily walk with God.*

And remember, *it's quality, not quantity, that counts:* better to think briefly about a single verse than to skim through pages without absorbing anything, because it's about developing your relationship with the living God. The sign that your daily time with God is real is when you start to love him more and serve him more wholeheartedly.

Tim Thornborough and Carl Laferton
Editors

1 PETER: Persevering in pain

When the Christian life feels like a struggle we can wonder: "Have we somehow made a mistake? Have we misunderstood God's plans for us and this world?"

Peter writes to reassure Christians to stick to God's unchanged pattern for our lives and plans for the world.

God's pattern for life

Read 1 Peter 5:12

It's often helpful to look at the end of a letter to find out the writer's motivation for penning it. It's certainly true in the case of 1 Peter. We find in 5:12 a summary sentence that gives us a steer as to what the main aim of his letter is.

- ❓ *How does Peter describe his readers' circumstances and their beliefs?*
- ❓ *How then should they respond to their situation?*

God's plan for the world

Read 1 Peter 1:1-2

1 Peter was written to Christians scattered around Asia Minor which is now modern day Turkey. They knew hardship and struggle as daily realities.

- ❓ *How should they consider their situation in the world (v 1)?*
- ❓ *What certainty can they have about God's involvement in their lives?*

As Christians we belong to God (elect) and yet are strangers (exiles) in the world. We experience rejection and hostility because of our faith and lifestyle. Yet we have the comfort of knowing that the Holy Spirit has brought us to faith in Christ whose blood cleanses us from the guilt of sin.

⌄ Apply

- ❓ *What is the bigger struggle right now: knowing that God is involved in the difficult circumstances you face (5:12) or that this world is not your home (1:1)?*
- ❓ *How do God's words encourage you to persevere?*

⌃ Pray

Pray that God would help us to remember the momentous work that he has done to save us.

Ask God to help you to persevere through the trials of life.

Rejoicing in trials

All of us go through tough times as Christians. Peter reminds us why there is great hope in looking to God when we are going through times of difficulty.

Born into hope

Read 1 Peter 1:3

> ❓ *Why can we rejoice when we suffer (v 3)?*

The confidence that we have is because our hope is *living*. Just as Jesus has been raised from the dead, we have been raised to new spiritual life (new birth) which will one day culminate in new physical life (our living hope). It is not wishful thinking but a guaranteed reality. It is also not based on our performance but his mercy.

⌄ Apply

> ❓ *How does this affect how we think of God when we're going through tough times?*

Kept for heaven

An inheritance is typically something that comes to you after someone has died. In this case, the one who died has risen again! Peter reminds us what that inheritance is like.

Read 1 Peter 1:4-5

> ❓ *How is this inheritance different from an "earthly" inheritance (v 4)?*
> ❓ *How can we be sure that we will receive it according to Peter (v 5)?*

⌄ Apply

> ❓ *What difference could this make when we feel abandoned by God?*
> ❓ *How could these verses help us to keep rejoicing when we are struggling with our faith?*

···· **TIME OUT** ··

We often pass over praising God when we face tricky life situations. This passage challenges that perspective. Even in the midst of trials Peter's first response is praise.

⌃ Pray

> ❓ *Praise God for our new birth through the resurrection of Christ.*
> ❓ *Praise God the future inheritance that this new birth secures for us.*

 Bible in a year: Deuteronomy 16-18 • Acts 4:23-37

Purpose in Pain

Have you ever wondered, "why is this happening to me? What is God's plan in all of this?" Peter was writing to Christians who may well have been asking this very question.

His answer is that though what they were experiencing may have been painful, it was purposeful.

Refining faith

Read 1 Peter 1:6-9

> ❷ *Are our trials accidental or intentional?*
> ❷ *What is their purpose?*

A severe trial is sometimes called an "acid test." This term originated during times when gold was widely circulated. Nitric acid was applied to an object of gold to see if it was genuine or not. If it was fake, the acid decomposed it; if it was genuine, the gold was unaffected. The point of the acid wasn't to destroy the gold, it was to prove that it was genuine treasure.

Rewarded faith

Our trials not only reveal something about our faith, but they ensure an incredible celebration in the future. Just like the reward at the end of a gruelling marathon might be the medal at the finish line and the congratulations of friends, so there is reward at the end of our spiritual finish line.

Read 1 Peter 1:7-9

> ❷ *What do you think is meant by "praise, glory and honour" (v 7)?*
> ❷ *How are we comforted now in the midst of our trials (v 8-9)?*

Normally when we read words like praise, glory and honour, we rightly connect them with Jesus. But Peter is saying that we are the ones who gain praise, glory and honour. Because of our faithfulness during our trials in this life, we will share in the praise, glory and honour that belongs to our Lord. So we enjoy him now and will join in the praise of him later.

---- **TIME OUT** ----------------------------------

Take time to reflect on the privileged status Christians enjoy compared even to the prophets and the angels in verses 10-12. Despite sometimes being despised by society Peter wants to remind us of our privileged position.

☑ Apply

> ❷ *Have you seen your faith stand the test of difficulty?*
> ❷ *How should this encourage you?*
> ❷ *What motivation from these verses most encourages you to persevere in faith?*

☒ Pray

Ask God to help you to know that trials have purpose, even if it is not obvious to us at the time.

Pray that the prospect of our celebration with Christ at the end would keep us persevering in faith.

Threes and fours

The rest of this chapter is mainly taken up with a haunting and thought-provoking series of lists that illustrate some principles of wisdom.

Incomprehensible
Read Proverbs 30:18-19

As the writer looks around, he sees many things in nature that he cannot hope to understand: a bird's flight; how slithering snakes move on rock; how vessels move through the water; and exactly how meeting and dating a young woman works! But his lack of comprehension leads him not to frustration or depression, but to wonder and praise.

Science and human enquiry have answered many of these questions. We know something about the gripping scales on a snake, and fluid dynamics and the psychology and biology of humans. But we should never cease to be amazed and to wonder at the rich diversity, beauty and ingenious brilliance of God's creation.

Unbearable
Read Proverbs 30:20-23

❷ *What is it about these things that makes them unbearable?*

Do any of the categories fit you or someone you know? Then spend some time praying for yourself and for them...

Wise little creatures
Read Proverbs 30:24-28

❷ *What worthy features is he drawing our attention to in these observations?*

···· **TIME OUT** ····································

To the eyes of a pagan scientist, these things may be the blind forces of selection and evolution. But the truly wise discern that the God who created all things has woven into nature lessons for us. Nature is God's other book of revelation. So next time you go for a walk, look for lessons to illustrate biblical truth. You'll be amazed how much is there for the learning.

Four dignified creatures
Read Proverbs 30:29-31

❷ *What is Agur drawing our attention to?*
❷ *Why?*

Four outcomes
Read Proverbs 30:32-33

Proverbs constantly makes us face up to this inescapable truth: *actions have their outcomes.* As surely as a thump on the nose will cause it to bleed, so allowing anger to rule your life will embroil you in conflict. But verse 32 gives us good news. The situation is potentially recoverable. Even if you have been stupid, and thought yourself better than others, or have allowed your mind to devise "revenge schemes", you can do something about it

Focusing on holiness

Do you ever find yourself stuck when it comes to making progress in holiness?
Today, Peter will give us some powerful motivation to keep working at it...

The family way

Several members of my extended family are adopted. They would testify that when you find yourself brought into a new family, there are new family ways that you must begin to get used to. So it is when we are born again into God's family.

Read 1 Peter 1:13-16

❷ *What attitude should we have towards our life in general (v 13)?*
❷ *How should this affect our actions (v 14-16)?*

Drunk people are less aware of what is going on around them. By contrast, to be sober minded is to have a clear view of reality. Peter wants to remind us to always keep in mind the reality that Christ is coming back and we are his children.

Future grace

Read 1 Peter 1:17-21

❷ *What is it about the future that should encourage us to be holy (v 17)?*
❷ *How does being children of God affect our attitude to holiness (v 18-19)?*

✔ Apply

❷ *In what particular area of life do you need to grow in holiness?*
❷ *Which motivation for holiness most spurs you on right now:*
  • *Christ's future coming (v 13, 17)*
  • *Your present status as God's child (v 14-16) or,*
  • *God's past grace in Christ (v 18-19)?*

⌃ Pray

Ask God to help you make progress towards holiness.

Pray that the motivations that Peter gives us would spur you on.

The power of the Word

Our new birth is all God's work (1:3) but what part do we play in our faith and growth?

Purified

Peter now turns his attention to the stunning effects of believing the gospel he has just explored in v 18-21 on our character.

Read 1 Peter 1:22

> ❓ *How have we been purified?*
> ❓ *What was the result?*
> ❓ *What should we do now? Why?*

We often think of holiness as mainly about personal purity. We are growing in holiness if we can point to ways in which we have become more disciplined in our Bible reading or prayer or fighting specific sins. However, the *first* application Peter makes after speaking about holiness is about how we treat our brothers and sisters. In fact he says that love for our brothers and sisters in the church is a specific result of faith in Christ.

Empowered

Read 1 Peter 1:23

> ❓ *What does God use to effect change in our lives?*
> ❓ *How does it compare to the effects of natural seeds?*

Peter gives us an incredible motivation to keep making progress in holiness. Just like a seed is transformed into a flower, we are transformed by God's word. The difference is that our change is not temporary, destined to wilt and die, but permanent.

···· TIME OUT ····

Peter quotes from Isaiah 40:6-8 to make his point that God's incredible power dwarfs the impotence of human effort. A similar contrast is made in the New Testament in 1 Corinthians 15:50-54. We also see the power of God's word spelt out in Deuteronomy 31:9-13, and Hebrews 4:12.

Growing

Read 1 Peter 2:1-3

> ❓ *What are we to get rid of?*
> ❓ *What are we to get more of?*

Newborn babies are often desperate for a mother's milk. They instinctively know that it will do them good. Is that your experience?

⌃ Apply

> ❓ *What attitude should we have to God's word in light of these verses?*
> ❓ *What vice do you feel most in danger of falling into at the moment?*
> ❓ *How does this passage change our attitude to God's word?*

⌃ Pray

Give thanks for the privilege of having God's word at work in our lives.

Ask God's Spirit through his word to keep doing his transforming work.

Following Christ

To follow the teachings of scripture is to follow Christ. Jesus said "a servant is not greater than his master". Following him always brings privilege as well as persecution.

The life of Christ

As Peter encourages his readers to follow Christ he reminds them of the experience of their saviour when he was on earth.

Read 1 Peter 2:4

- ❓ *Who is the living stone?*
- ❓ *How is he treated by humans?*
- ❓ *How is he treated by God?*
- ❓ *In what way is our experience similar to his? (See also 1:1.)*

The life of the church

Having reminded them of how precious Christ is to his father, Peter points out how precious the church in Christ is to him too.

Read 1 Peter 2:5-6

- ❓ *What are we being built into?*
- ❓ *What task have we been given?*

In the past, if you wanted to meet with God you had to go to God's house, the temple. It could be far away, and God did not dwell there permanently. Now we all have access to God through Christ, wherever we are!

Likewise only a select few (the Levites) were allowed to work as priests in the temple bringing sacrifices to God. But now the whole church has the privilege of speaking and living for him in a special way.

···· **TIME OUT** ································

Peter quotes from various Old Testament

texts in verses 6-8 (Isaiah 28:16; Psalm 118:22; Isaiah 8:14) to describe how people 'stumble' over Christ, the most important 'stone,' and so face judgement, because they refuse to believe and obey him. They are responsible for this and yet God had also planned it. We see this same pattern at the cross (Acts 2:23). Evil men carried out their own evil desires and yet God stood behind the flow of history as well. Although logically difficult to understand it is comforting when we experience suffering to know that God remains in ultimate control.

✔ Apply

- ❓ *How does remembering the life of Jesus spur us on when we face persecution?*
- ❓ *How does knowing that God is with us help in the midst of persecution?*
- ❓ *Do we spend as much time thinking about our status before God as we do our status in society?*

▲ Pray

Pray with thanks for the privileges of having God's presence permanently with us and the responsibility of speaking for him as his priests.

Ask God to help us to remember the privilege of following in the footsteps of Christ when we face persecution for our faith.

Privileged to praise

Christians are called to a special relationship with God. Before any sense of duty comes a unique distinction

Chosen for privilege

This passage echoes Exodus 19 where having been led out of Egypt, God declares how special his people are to him.

Read 1 Peter 2:9-10

> ❷ *Which description most excites you?*
> ❷ *How do Christians obtain this status?*

When Peter was writing, Christians would have been on the margins of political and social life. There was little prospect of the church becoming popular or attractive to the culture at large. It would have been a comfort to remember that their status in the eyes of God is very different from their status in the eyes of the world.

Chosen for praise

> ❷ *What is it Christians are to do (v 9)?*
> ❷ *How does v 10 help us with this task?*

The blessings God has showered on us are for a purpose. Peter draws on the language of the Psalms (e.g. Psalm 18:49; 57:9; 105:1) to point out that we are called to direct our praises to the nations.

···· **TIME OUT** ···································

Peter is using familiar Old Testament passages to make his point (especially Exodus 19:3-6; Hosea 2:23; Isaiah 43:20-21). The church now takes on the privileges that the people of Israel were given.

☑ Apply

> ❷ *How can we remember the role that God has given us?*
> ❷ *Why should praise flow naturally?*
> ❷ *What could we do when we feel less inclined to talk about Jesus?*

▲ Pray

Pray that we would rejoice in the privileges that God has given us in Christ

Ask God for fresh insight into these privileges that causes us to regularly want to praise him too others

Peculiar praise

Often our journey to faith involves significant relationships with Christians. A common theme in our testimonies is that "there was something about them that was different".

What should "different" look like for Christians?

Self control

Read 1 Peter 2:11

> ❓ *What words does Peter use to describe us?*

The language of being in a foreign place is meant to remind us that much of what goes on around us should be unfamiliar and out of step with what we should consider as normal for our new life as Christian community.

> ❓ *What does Peter encourage us to do?*
> ❓ *According to his description, will it be easy?*

Doing good

Read 1 Peter 2:12

> ❓ *What do we start doing?*

Our good behaviour doesn't replace the good news that people must hear and believe to become a Christian. How we live cannot save someone. But it can make our message much more attractive.

> ❓ *What can the effect of good deeds be on people's attitude to our faith?*

Peter's thought fits well with 3:15. There he encourages us to be ready to explain the reason for our hope when people ask why

we do good deeds. Our distinctive behaviour is meant to cause curiosity.

✔ Apply

> ❓ *Where do you need to exercise more self control?*
> ❓ *Who could you talk to about this?*
> ❓ *In what area of life do you interact most with non Christians e.g. sport, work, leisure time?*
> ❓ *How could your actions be most distinct in that setting?*

⌃ Pray

Pray for the Lord's help to live good lives.

Pray for others in areas where you are finding it hard to be self controlled.

Pray that others would find our lifestyle as a community attractive.

Listening to our leaders

Election campaigns can be a time when Christians either disengage from politics or become very partisan. What does the Bible actually say about government?

Submitting

Read 1 Peter 2:13-14

- ❓ *What should our attitude to governments be?*
- ❓ *How do individuals come to hold positions of power?*
- ❓ *What is their role according to Peter?*

⌄ Apply

- ❓ *What difference does understanding God's role in government make when we face elections?*
- ❓ *How could we show honour to our government in our speech?*
- ❓ *In what way might this shape our attitude to government during and after the Covid-19 pandemic?*

···· TIME OUT ·····································

Peter doesn't address the issue of unjust governments. Jesus was happy to publicly call out bad behaviour in political life when it was necessary e.g. Luke 13:32. Paul, likewise, can call us to pray for our leaders (1 Timothy 2:1-2) and yet call out the unjust practises that they endorse like slave trading (1 Timothy 1:10). It does however seem to lay out a default attitude of respect towards those in authority.

Silencing scoffers

Read 1 Peter 2:15-17

It seems that Paul was worried about Christians becoming disorderly and disobedient. It is sometimes the case that if people reject the ultimate authority of government they descend into anarchy.

- ❓ *How should our behaviour counter fears of the government (v 15)?*
- ❓ *What should we avoid (v 16)?*

The attitude of honour doesn't just stop with governments. Peter says that we should honour everyone— every single person we come across.

⌄ Apply

- ❓ *What might it look like to have a good reputation with our landlords when renting a flat?*
- ❓ *How could our behaviour show that we seek to honour everyone when:*
  - *you're in a restaurant?*
  - *you're speaking to a delivery driver?*
  - *you're interacting with school or college teachers?*

⌃ Pray

Pray for God's help to remember that governments are ordained by God.

Ask for God's help to submit to the leadership of our government.

The emptiness of wisdom

Lemuel (and presumably his mum, who taught him) does not appear to have been a king of Israel. So how is it that his words have ended up in the Bible?

God gives "common grace". He showers his blessings on all mankind—even those who do not acknowledge him. And much of the world's wisdom is sound enough. It is testimony to God's remarkable sovereignty that many parts of the Bible were written and collected by those who were unaware that they were doing God's bidding. But what we have at last is, every bit of it, God's word.

Leadership qualities
Read Proverbs 31:1-9

❓ *What three areas do leaders particularly need to be careful of (v 3, 4, 8-9)?*

These three have a continuing modern ring to them—not just in the political arena, but for those in spiritual leadership as well. How often has Satan used sex, drink and the abuse of power as the primary means of bringing down ministries and whole churches? Not surprising then that in the New Testament, moral strength in these areas are the prerequisite for those who would serve in the churches of God.

🔼 Pray

Read Titus 1:5-9 and then pray for the leaders in your own church: pastors, home-group leaders, those who teach children and young people, etc. Pray that God would help them to resist the pull of these temptations. Pray for yourself also that you would be vig-ilant to spot signs of danger, and to humbly help them.

Pray that you would be strong enough to follow the encouragement of **Galatians 6:1-2.**

Who you represent
Re-read Proverbs 31:8-9

The first calling of the leader is to be a servant—to the poor, the needy, and for those who are mute—who can't speak for themselves.

Worldly leadership will gather about itself an in-crowd of the elite. The truly wise leader, however, will champion and gather to himself the lowly, the outcasts, the victims of abuse, the poor and the needy.

❓ *Does this remind you of anyone? (See Luke 14:12-24 for a King who did this.)*

🔼 Pray

Give praise to our great wise King Jesus, who judges with righteousness and who welcomes the poor and needy—yes, even you.

Working Life

What do you do if, day after day, your boss is difficult to work with but you have no immediate way of changing your situation?

Freedom in fragility

Despite telling his readers of their freedom to follow God (2:16), the circumstances of many were often complex. The slavery in view in the Roman Empire was not racialised and was sometimes voluntary in order to earn citizenship or to pay off debt. But they still had little honour and were at the mercy of the attitude of their masters. Many were in situations that left them with a choice between sinful anger and righteous endurance.

Read 1 Peter 2:18-20

> ❓ *How did Peter encourage slaves to respond to their masters?*
> ❓ *In what situations was this expected?*
> ❓ *What were they to avoid?*
> ❓ *What motivation does he give for this?*

Peter isn't condoning the system, but recognising that some of those he is writing to are powerless to do anything to change their situation. They must know what it means to live Christianly in their circumstances.

⌄ Apply

> ❓ *How might this apply in a difficult work environment?*
> ❓ *What might it look to "bear up" in a non-ideal situation even while seeking to change it?*

···· TIME OUT ······························

Peter's theology refutes the idea that some

people are inherently inferior which fuelled the institution of slavery. He refers to all his readers (including slaves) as "free" (v 16). He emphasises that honour is due to all (v 17) and unlike other ethical codes at the time, he addresses slaves as responsible moral agents (v 18). In other words, slaves were and are precious people who are worthy of the same dignity as anyone else.

Freedom to follow

The next section is not just directed at household servants. Peter sees the household slave situation as a case study for the whole household of faith. So he gives all his readers motivation to stand firm under unjust suffering.

Read 1 Peter 2:21-25

> ❓ *How did Jesus act and think when he faced unjust suffering (v 21-23)?*
> ❓ *What did his unjust death achieve (v 24-25)?*
> ❓ *How might Jesus' death shape our response to injustices that are beyond our power to influence?*

⌃ Pray

Pray for persevering grace when we face unjust suffering that we can't easily escape.

Ask God to strengthen Christians in a country where persecution is more severe than your own with these truths.

True beauty

In a world of makeup advertisements and surgically enhanced bodies, what does God's word have to say about what it means to be truly beautiful?

Mission focussed

Read 1 Peter 3:1

❓ *What were Peter's instructions designed to help achieve?*

❓ *What was the key instruction? Which "husbands" are in mind?*

This section continues a big theme of surprising a sceptical world that marginalises Christians, with surprising behaviour (see 2:11-12). A chief characteristic is submission (2:13, 18; 3:1, 5; 5:5) and it is not merely directed at women. To Western ears "submit" seems like an alien and oppressive concept. But Peter's main thrust here is that Christians should recognise the status that others had in society at the time and not seek to usurp it. In this way the gospel would not be discredited.

Inwardly focussed

Read 1 Peter 3:2-4

❓ *What kind of "adornment" will not win an unbelieving husband to Christ?*

❓ *What might?*

❓ *What kind of beauty does God value? (See also Isaiah 66:2; 1 Samuel 16:2.)*

❓ *What has the power to draw unbelieving husbands to Christ is not a woman's looks but her lifestyle.*

Other focussed

Read 1 Peter 3:5-7

❓ *What are the chief strengths that women should cultivate (v 6)?*

Peter is in no way condoning becoming a victim of abuse but encouraging wives to remain loyal to Christ. As he has said in 2:17 we are all to show love and respect to everyone and yet to fear God above all else.

❓ *How should Christian husbands make all of this easier to do?*

⌄ Apply

❓ *How do Peter's words affect your approach to beauty?*

❓ *What would it look like to put this passage into practice in your life?*

❓ *In what ways do you find this a challenge and an encouragement?*

⌃ Pray

Pray for wives married to non-Christian husbands to be able to live distinct lives that point to Christ.

Ask God to help Christian husbands to be continually aware of the divine gift that their wives are and to treat them with honour and care.

A community of peace

In a world of insults and dismissive attitudes, our ability to keep going is really helped by having close relationships within our Christian community.

Peacemaking attitudes

Peter echoes the book of Philippians in calling for Christian communities to stick together so that they do not face persecution alone (Philippians 1:27-28).

Read 1 Peter 3:8

> ❷ *How could a compassionate community be a help when facing insults?*
> ❷ *How could a humble attitude help us cope with criticism?*

☑ Apply

> ❷ *Which one of these characteristics (compassion or humility) feels more of a challenge in your relationships at church right now?*

Peacemaking choices

In this verse we hear echoes of Jesus in the Sermon on the Mount as Peter encourages us to seek peace.

Read 1 Peter 3:9

> ❷ *What choices should we try to make when we are wronged in our church community?*

Just as when Paul called the Philippians to compassion (Philippians 2:1) and humility (2:3), our chief example is Christ who humbled himself for us (2:8). Peter has lagged this too in 1 Peter 2:21-24.

☑ Apply

> ❷ *In which relationship in church life is this a choice that you need to nurture at the moment?*

Listening God

In verse 9 peacemaking appears to lead to blessing. To explain this, Peter quotes from Psalm 34. In that Psalm, the blessing in view comes in the midst of trouble. That means that the blessing is neither our troubles vanishing or merely life after death.

Read 1 Peter 3:10-12

> ❷ *What blessings does Peter highlight in verses 10 and 12?*

It seems that the blessing that Peter had in mind is our awareness of God's presence and his attentiveness to our prayers. In other words, the fellowship and life with God that comes from our new birth, starting now (2:24) and extending into eternity (3:7). In other words peacemaking is simply an integral part of life for God's blessed people.

⌃ Pray

Pray that God would help you to grow in showing compassion and humility in church life.

Ask God to help you to identify relationships that may be in need of repair.

The right kind of fear

We live in a world that is increasingly hostile to the Christian message. How do we seek to make Christ known when nobody seems to want to hear?

The right preparation
Read 1 Peter 3:13-16

❷ *What should we be prepared for (v 13-14)?*
❷ *What should we be ready to do (v 15-16)?*

Peter presumes that, as Christians revere (or fear) God above everything else, the distinctiveness of our lifestyles will start to raise questions in people's minds.

⌄ Apply

❷ *How is this an encouragement in a world that seems hostile to Christianity?*
❷ *How could you be more prepared to answer people's questions?*

The right perspective
Read 1 Peter 3:17-22

❷ *What has Jesus done for us (v 18)?*
❷ *What happened to him in the end (v 18)?*

Peter's point here is that in the life of Jesus, victory followed apparent defeat. Christ's victory included not only being "made alive" in the resurrection but declaring his victory and his enemies' defeat in the spiritual realm. Our baptism reminds us that, like Noah in the Old Testament, we get caught up in this victory. As we pledge to follow God by faith, our baptism symbolises how we are saved from judgement.

···· TIME OUT ································

The broad consensus on the meaning of verses 19-20 is that, sometime after his resurrection, Christ proclaimed his victory to fallen angels, imprisoned since the time of Noah. His victory reiterated their defeat. The background to this is found in Genesis 6:1-4 and the extra biblical material found in the inter-testamental book of 1 Enoch, which would have been familiar to Peter's readers.

⌄ Apply

❷ *How is the pattern of Jesus' life an inspiration for us?*
❷ *How do Jesus' actions encourage us to keep putting him first?*

Living for God

"I want to stand up for Jesus but I'm worried about the backlash that might come my way." Most of us have thought like this at one time or other.

And Peter understands that temptation too. So he writes to encourage us to have the right attitude when it comes to suffering for Jesus.

The right attitude to God's will

Read 1 Peter 3:18 and 4:1-2

> ❷ *What did Christ's suffering do to our sin (3:18)?*
> ❷ *How are we to live now (4:1-2)?*

Christians choose to live a new kind of life, made possible by Christ (2:24) and marked by our baptism (3:21) .

The right attitude to sin

Read 1 Peter 4:3-6

> ❷ *What should our attitude be to our previous way of life (v 3)?*
> ❷ *How will some people view us (v 4)?*
> ❷ *How can remembering the future help us to stand firm in our convictions (v 5)?*

Peter points out in verse 6 that the same salvation that we look forward to applies to believers who heard the gospel and subsequently died. Though they may appear to face the same earthly fate and so are "judged according to human standards," their spiritual reality is entirely different. Their contemporaries may have poured scorn on them, but they will be vindicated in the end.

Apply

❷ *What are some of the modern equivalents of the list in verse 3?*
❷ *Do you ever feel pressured to conform to the standards of those around you?*
❷ *Are you prepared to take the abuse that comes from living for Christ?*

Pray

For strength to keep living for Christ.

For courage to speak up for him even when we might get flack for it.

For those whose stand for Christ brings the family rejection, imprisonment or worse.

Living in light of the end

As aliens and strangers in the world, we should expect some people to be surprised by and even abusive about our lifestyle (4:4). How we respond is important for us and for others.

Vertical focus

Read 1 Peter 4:4:7

❓ *What do we need to remember?*
❓ *How should we act as a result?*

Peter explains that "all things"—that is all the main historical events required before Jesus' return to judge (v 5) and to reveal his glory (v 13), have already happened. This should concentrate our minds on the way we are living now, whether this takes place next Monday or next millennium.

···· **TIME OUT** ········

St Benedict once said: "keep death always before your eyes." His aim wasn't to walk through life sad, but exactly the opposite. This kind of reflection focussed his mind on meeting Jesus and consciously using the time before that meeting in ways that were most profitable.

Horizontal focus

Living in light of the end doesn't just affect our relationship with God (v 7) but with others too (v 8-11).

Read 1 Peter 4:8-11

❓ *What kind of attitude should we have towards one another?*
❓ *How do we express this?*

⌄ Apply

❓ *How does focussing on Jesus' return affect our attitude to life?*
❓ *In which of the ways listed in verses 8-11 has God particularly gifted you to serve your local church?*
❓ *How could you bless people with this in the next few days?*
❓ *Who have you seen show gifting in one of these areas? How could you encourage them to bless others with their gift?*
❓ *Do you struggle more with self importance or self doubt when it comes to serving God?*
❓ *How does being a steward of God's grace, empowered by God's strength (v 10-11) correct our thinking?*

⌃ Pray

Pray that God would help us to see life through the lens of the end.

Ask God to help you to continue to serve your brother's and sisters in church with love.

Ask the Lord to help you see how you might bless his church worldwide.

A godly wife...

Take the time to think about this passage properly. Some women can feel a little insulted by it's content, and some men can use it as an unhelpful measure for others.

❓ *If you had to list the top five qualities you are looking for in a wife or husband, what would they be?*

❓ *What are the qualities that this passage praises? How do your lists compare?*

This famous poem that brings the book of Proverbs to a close is an "acrostic" in the original language—each line begins with the next letter of the alphabet.

Notice that many of the things that we might have thought to include in the list above do not appear! There's not much about "romantic love" or a sense of humour, (although she does laugh at the future in verse 25). In particular there is *nothing at all* about how she looks.

Superwoman?

❓ *Write down what you think are the top qualities of this idealised woman that the poem is saying are desirable.*

❓ *What does verse 30 say to men looking for a bride, and women wanting to be a bride?*

Maybe there are more important things than sex drive when choosing a partner! And surely the first thing has to be that they love (and fear) the Lord. The quality that starts Proverbs (1:7) also finishes it. All her many qualities and accomplishments—hard work, business sense, reliability, kindness—*all* of them stem ultimately from her relationship with God.

Some women (and men) may be rather intimidated by this vision of a modern, multi-tasking, highly capable, businesslike wife. But read deeper into the poem, and we see that this is the wife of a community leader (31:23), and that she sets him free to do his work, while managing the children and the household. Although her achievements are many, her focus is on her husband and children, to serve and enable them in a wonderful partnership. But this not a loveless, functionally efficient marriage, where the woman is invisible. There is love, honour and respect from everyone: husband, children and the community at large—all hold this woman in high regard (v 11-12, 28-29).

⌄ Apply

We don't have a parallel poem about a godly husband. Perhaps this is here *mainly* for Adams to read, and repent of their wrong thinking about what is truly desirable in a potential or actual Eve.

❓ *How might a version aimed at a man read? What would be different?*

⌃ Pray

Praise God for the many fine, capable and hard-working women, both single and married, in your church. Pray that they would be appreciated, and that you would have an opportunity to thank and honour them.

 Bible in a year: Psalms 20-22 • Acts 13:26-52

A checklist for sufferers

Peter returns again to the theme of suffering as a Christian. Here we get a helpful summary of what to think and what to do .

What to think in suffering
Read 1 Peter 4:12-14

- ❓ *How should we think about our circumstances when we experience suffering (v 12)?*
- ❓ *In what ways should we be encouraged (v 13-14)?*

It's striking that even fiery ordeals should not surprise us but cause us to rejoice! We are reminded that when we share in the pattern of Christ's life now, we will also share in it in resurrection glory. What's more, we are aware of the power of the Holy Spirit in a special way.

What to check in suffering
Read 1 Peter 4:15-16

- ❓ *When might we be suffering from the wrong reasons (v 15)?*

When Peter talks of judgement in verse 17 he is calling to mind how God sorts people into groups—those who belong to him and those who don't. He has already explained in 1:6-7 that one way that he does this work is through trials. He hints that he has the same idea in mind in 4:12 when he talks about how trials "test" us. Our suffering and perseverance for Christ then demonstrate that God has placed us among his saved people.

What to do in suffering
Read 1 Peter 4:19

- ❓ *How should we respond in suffering?*

✔ Apply

- ❓ *Are there character traits that you need to address that invite suffering for the wrong reasons?*
- ❓ *Are there ways that we find ourselves trying to avoid suffering for what is right personally?*
- ❓ *What has most encouraged you from verses 12-19 to persevere in suffering?*

✦ Pray

Ask God for confidence to live and speak for Jesus even if it might bring hostility.

Pray that God would help you to recall the privilege of suffering for Christ and trust in Him in times of persecution.

Shepherd leadership

Peter assumes that among his listeners will be elders and lay people from different churches. How should they organise themselves in their new situation?

Shepherding the flock
Read 1 Peter 5:1-2

❷ *What responsibility do elders have?*
❷ *How should they go about the task?*

Peter's teaching challenges much modern leadership thinking. Before a pastor is a platform speaker or engaged in community transformation or acting like anything approaching a CEO, he is a shepherd.

Following the chief shepherd
Read 1 Peter 4:3-4

❷ *What motivations does Peter give for the type of leadership in verses 1-2?*
❷ *How is verse 4 an encouragement when leading beleaguered congregations?*

Just like the ministry of Jesus, earthly ministry may be full of struggle, but glory is guaranteed when Christ returns (see 1:13).

···· TIME OUT ·································

As he does throughout the letter, Peter seems to pick up here on his own personal experiences with Jesus. Not only did he witness the suffering of Jesus first hand, but he also heard his teaching. Jesus encouraged his disciples to avoid vying for position (Mark 9:33-37) and lording it over others in leadership but instead to be humble servants (Mark 10:42-45).

⌄ Apply

❷ *How then do you spot a good pastor according to Peter?*
❷ *What should we pray for our pastors?*
❷ *How could we encourage our pastors with these truths?*

⌃ Pray

Pray that the elders of your church (whether they go by this name or not) would embody these characteristics.

Pray that whether you are a leader in your church or not, the motivation for ministry would remain the reward of Christ himself.

Humble community

Having pointed out the importance of the role of elders in our local churches, Peter unpacks the secret to living well in community

Humility towards others

Read 1 Peter 5:5

> ❓ *How should we relate to our leaders?*
> ❓ *What kind of attitude will help us to relate well to everyone?*

It is important to note that submitting to leaders becomes possible when they are behaving as the servant leaders Peter has just described in verses 1-3. But this is just one aspect of the attitude that "all" should have to one another. God's design, as expressed in the quote from Proverbs 3:34, is to favour the humble.

Humility towards God

Read 1 Peter 5:6-7

> ❓ *What does Peter want us to realise about who controls our circumstances (v 6)?*
> ❓ *How do we demonstrate a humble attitude before God (v 7)?*

Peter echoes the teaching of Jesus who says: "those who exalt themselves will be humbled, and those who humble themselves will be exalted," (Matthew 23:12). This is not meant to lead to competitiveness among Christians. It is simply a basic attitude of discipleship.

Pride is sometimes described as a little bit like limescale in a kettle. It stops it responding as well as it should. Similarly, our pride can make it harder for us to respond to others and to God as we should. Thankfully God gives us a means to cultivate the right attitude—we can remove the "limescale" of pride through prayer.

⌄ Apply

> ❓ *When are you least convinced that you have anything to learn from God?*
> ❓ *When do you find yourself resistant to the ideas of others?*
> ❓ *How could reflecting on our 'smallness' and God's might help our humility?*
> ❓ *Do you first bring your anxieties to God or try to solve them yourself?*

⌃ Pray

Ask that God might grow a spirit of humility among your whole church community.

Pray that as a church community you would become more prayerful.

Share with the Lord the ways in which you need his help in the situation he has put you in right now.

Resisting the devil

Behind the insults and persecutions that Christians endure lies the slander and hostility of a supernatural enemy.

Know your enemy
Read 1 Peter 5:8

- ❷ *Who should we be aware of?*
- ❷ *Why is this important?*
- ❷ *How do you think that the imagery of a lion in verse 8 relates to the care of "the flock" in verses 1-4?*

There is more going on when we face hostility than mere unkindness. There is a supernatural enemy to contend with as well. While we all have a role of resistance in the face of the devil's activity, pastors have a particular role to resist for the sake for the flock.

···· **TIME OUT** ··························

What does faithful resistance to the devil look like? Perhaps we get a clue from the book of James. "Submission to God" (James 4:6-7) seems to overlap with Peter's theme of humility. One of the devil's chief strategies is to incite pride in us. We need to place ourselves under the mighty hand of God whatever happens—and however tempted we are to think that we are capable and that "we can fix this".

Remember your family
Read 1 Peter 5:9

- ❷ *What does Peter encourage us to do?*
- ❷ *What do we need to remember?*

Praise God that none of us suffer or resist alone, since there are many across the globe who suffer similarly. Reading about missionaries from the past and praying for persecuted Christians in the present can help us to remain mindful of this.

⌃ Pray

For a daily awareness of the presence and reality of the evil one.

Ask God to help you resist evil by humbly trusting in God and remembering that we are not alone.

Pray that you would be vigilant for those who might be vulnerable to being "devoured" by the devil—perhaps even you.

The reward for resistance

Having encouraged us to resist the devil, Peter shares some wonderful rewards that await those who stand firm.

Suffering is temporary

Read 1 Peter 5:10

> ❓ *How long is our suffering for?*
> ❓ *Who will ensure that our suffering ends?*

Peter is not saying that our suffering will necessarily be brief, but that an earthly lifetime is only a little while compared with eternity. Our confidence of this future comes not from our loyalty to God but his faithfulness to us.

☑ Apply

> ❓ *How does eternity make sense of the Christian life, when our suffering seems never ending?*

Reward awaits

Read 1 Peter 5:10-14

> ❓ *What promises of future blessing does Peter give (v 10)?*

Even though we may know suffering is temporary we can still feel weakened and damaged by it. Here God offers us hope. The Lord will restore us by putting all things right. He will make us strong in the faith—empowering us when before we have felt weak. And he will make us firm and steadfast—with unshakeable security in Christ's presence.

> ❓ *How can the nature of God's power encourage us under trial (v 11)?*

At the time of writing it must have looked to most people that the Roman Empire had all the power, with all the iron-fisted threat which that brought for Christians. In fact says Peter, despite appearances, the power of God reigns supreme.

☑ Apply

> ❓ *How do God's promises for the future help us to stand firm in faith now when we face persecution?*
> ❓ *What does remembering God's present power add to this in persecution?*

☑ Pray

Ask God to impress upon your heart the reality of these future promises.

Pray that when facing suffering we would be conscious that God has not lost control.

A godly wife ... take II

We're going back one more time to the end of Proverbs to see that there is a deeper current of meaning here if we look carefully at it.

Looking deeper
Read Proverbs 31:10-31

> ❓ Who is the woman in this poem married to (v 23)?
> ❓ What is the picture of a bride or a wife frequently used to represent in the Bible?
> ❓ So how might we read a deeper meaning in this famous passage?

Throughout scripture, God is pictured as a husband to who has taken to himself a bride who he chose, and whom he loves. Think of the book of Hosea, or this beautiful image from Isaiah 54:4:

"For your Maker is your husband, the Lord of hosts is his name; and the Holy One of Israel is your Redeemer, the God of the whole earth he is called."

Genesis reveals that the first man and woman were made jointly in the image of God, and that there is something particularly profound and revealing of the nature of God as two become one.

In the New Testament, the full extent of all that God purposed in our sexual duality is revealed: Christ is the husband who joins himself to his bride—his people—forever.

TIME OUT
Read Ephesians 5:21-32

> ❓ What is the "profound mystery" that Paul is talking about here?
> ❓ Is this how you think about marriage?

Being the godly wife

So it is possible to read this whole chapter as a description of what it means to be joined to Jesus—both as an individual, and as a local and universal church.

Read Proverbs 31:10-31 again

> ❓ What jumps out at you as a description of how you and your church should be known as "married to Jesus".

She is a worker, she is creative, she is a carer—constantly active to promote and honour her husband and the family. She expends herself from early to late, making sure that the household of faith is nurtured and cared for and properly "fed".

> ❓ Is that a good description of your church?
> ❓ Is that a good description of you?
> ❓ What aspect of her diligence do you think you could aspire more to?

Pray

Ask the Lord to make you such a bride!

Ask God to help you be more proactive in growing his kingdom.

And pray that your church would be known and honoured for its hard work, devotion to the family, and for the way it's love flows outward to the poor and needy in the community.

I've started so I'll finish

We've come to the end of a long haul through Proverbs, but it would be worthwhile taking a moment to reflect on how God wants us to live "the Good Life".

The Proverbs principle

Read Proverbs 1:1-7

❓ *What should you have gained in working through Proverbs as we have done?*

❓ *What does verse 7 tell us is the key to thinking and living in a genuinely wise way?*

It's a long book, and sometimes quite difficult to take in when we read a long section. But the wonderful thing about this book, as we have repeatedly said, is that it's not a list of commands to be learned and slavishly obeyed to the letter. It is a set of potential outworkings from a very simple principle. If we genuinely "fear the LORD" we can never go far wrong.

We are told in 1 Kings 4:32 that Solomon spoke 3,000 proverbs. The book of Proverbs doesn't even come close to containing that many. In its 31 chapters there are only around 800. And many of these are about the antithesis of wisdom: *folly.*

❓ *Why is it so important that we think clearly about what "un-wisdom" is, as well as seeing examples of true wisdom?*

The proverbs that were recorded for us, and which we have read through are not the last word on wise living. To live wisely, we must genuinely know God as revealed in Christ through the scriptures. And we must understand how we relate to him as Lord

and lover, as the thoroughly imperfect who was chosen, loved and called by the utterly perfect. This is the place from which we can apply wisdom, as we are guided by his Spirit and informed by the mind of Christ.

❓ *What issues of wise living are you facing at the moment? In your...*
- *work?*
- *relationships?*
- *church?*
- *family?*

❓ *How will you reach a tentative conclusion on how to act wisely?*

⌄ Apply

It is wise always to seek counsel from trusted friends and older Christians, and our conclusions from the Proverbs principle must never conflict with the plain commands of scripture. But God does give us considerable freedom to act as we perceive to be the way of wisdom, and more than that, he delights in our choices as we walk humbly before him. When we fear God, we have nothing to fear.

⌃ Pray

Thank God for the freedom and joy there is in serving him.

And pray that you would walk and live in confidence before him.

EZEKIEL: My holy name

Do you ever get depressed thinking about the weakness of the church and the strength of those who oppose God? Does it ever make you doubt? Does God really make a difference?

Israel has been defeated by the Babylonians. Its leaders are in exile (Daniel included). Ezekiel who is a young priest, is now far from his beloved temple. Babylon is top dog and Israel is just one of many vassal kingdoms. Are the gods of Babylon greater than the God of Israel? Is Israel's God impotent? Or maybe he no longer cares?

A God without limits
Read Ezekiel 1:1-14

> ❓ *What does Ezekiel see? Can you picture it in your mind's eye?*

Ezekiel sees a vision of God—and what a vision! Flashing lightning, brilliant light, glowing metal, supernatural creatures, wonderful jewels. All these details reinforce the message that God is great and holy and glorious. And what Ezekiel saw was only "the appearance of the likeness of the glory of LORD" (v 28)—it wasn't even the real thing!

A God without borders
Read Ezekiel 1:15-24

> ❓ *What does Ezekiel see now? Can you picture it in your mind's eye?*
> ❓ *What do you think this strange sight means?*

The God of Israel is also the sovereign Lord of the world—even in Babylon! He meets

with Ezekiel by a Babylonian river (verses 1 and 3). And his throne is mobile. He's not rooted to the spot. The movement of the creatures and the wheels symbolises God's rule over all the earth, even in Babylon, even in the darkest parts of your town, even in the most remote parts of the world. And the rim full of eyes (v 18) is a reminder that God sees the plight of his people.

A God who is human
Read Ezekiel 1:25-28

> ❓ *What's the big surprise in verse 26?*
> ❓ *How did Ezekiel respond to his vision?*

At the heart of this vision is "a figure like that of a man" God is human—not as we are, but as we should be. Ezekiel's vision of God's glory shapes his ministry (he often refers back to it). The book has a refrain repeated some 60 times: "Then they will know that I am the LORD". The gospel in Ezekiel is not man-centred, but God-centred. It is not about God helping us out, giving us fulfilment or enabling us to reach our potential. It is about God establishing the holiness and honour of his name in judgment and in salvation.

⌃ Pray

Use the imagery of Ezekiel 1 to praise God. Meditate on Revelation 1:12-18.

Speak to the hand

Sometimes in our studies on Ezekiel, only a selection of verses will be chosen. Those who want to read the whole passage should also read the verses in brackets.

The task
Read Ezekiel 2:1-7 (3:4-7)

> ❓ *What is Ezekiel commissioned to do?*
> ❓ *What response will he get?*

It is hardly the most motivational call to evangelism. Ezekiel is told to speak to people who just *will not listen*. Though God speaks (2:4), they will not listen. It is not that they cannot understand what is said—it's not obscure or difficult (3:6). The problem is that they will not accept God's word. It is a problem of will, not a problem of understanding.

···· **TIME OUT** ····································

Read 2 Corinthians 2:14-16

God's word brings life to some, but it also hardens others in their rebellion. It is sometimes said that modern science makes Christian faith untenable. But the problem is not that the message is untenable, but that people will not accept it. It is a problem of the heart rather than the mind.

> ❓ *How might this affect the way we share the gospel?*

The messenger
Read Ezekiel 2:8 – 3:3

> ❓ *What encouragements does Ezekiel receive that will sustain him?*

> ❓ *How does God equip him for his work (see 3:8-13, 22-27)?*

God calls Ezekiel to the task of speaking to those who will not listen. But how does God encourage and equip Ezekiel—and us?

- God's word will sustain us. And it will keep us from sharing the rebellion of those among whom we live and serve.
- God will strengthen us and be with us so there is no need to be afraid (v 8-9).
- God reminds us of his glory (v 22-23).
- God enables us to speak(v 24-27).

> ❓ *How did Ezekiel respond to his commission (see v 14-15)?*

Accountable to God
Read Ezekiel 3:16-21

We can't make someone believe—they're responsible for how they respond to the gospel. But we are responsible for sharing the gospel with those we can.

🔼 Pray

Maybe you feel like Ezekiel did—over-whelmed and deeply distressed by the task before us? Ask God to strengthen you and sustain you by his word, by the comfort of being close to others, and with a greater vision of God's greatness.

The theatre of doom

This all has a very modern sense of the avant garde about it. Ezekiel is about to act out the fate of Israel in a series of bizarre pieces of "performance art".

Model prophet
Read Ezekiel 4:1-17

> ❷ *What does God call him to do, and what does it all mean?*
> ❷ *How long will this acted message last?*
> ❷ *What does Ezekiel push back on, and how does God respond (v 12)?*

Ezekiel must make a model of Jerusalem besieged and then lie prostrate under the burden of Israel and Judah's sin—for over a year! God tells Ezekiel to eat defiled food (something abhorrent to a devoted Israelite) to show what God's people will be forced to do, under siege and in exile. But he draws the line at the final instruction having to cook it using human excrement! God spares Ezekiel what he, and presumably his onlookers, would have thought extremely offensive. This horrible and distasteful display is intended to evoke in the onlookers the same horror they will feel at the plight to come because of their sin (v 17).

☑ Apply

Some Christians are suspicious of "different" types of communication.

> ❷ *Is there anything we can learn from the way God told Ezekiel to spread his message?*
> ❷ *How might you use alternative forms of communication to share the gospel with family and friends, rather than words?*

Hair-raising
Read Ezekiel 5

> ❷ *What "performance piece" does God instruct Ezekiel to enact now?*
> ❷ *What does it all mean?*

Ezekiel's own hair is a picture of God's people. Some will be burnt, some will be cut down by the sword and some will be scattered. Even the few that remain will suffer further afflictions. And in case you didn't get the point, God explains the meaning. He placed Jerusalem "in the centre of the nations" to be a light to those nations (v 5); to witness to the goodness of his rule. But the people of Jerusalem didn't keep the law of God. Instead of being a light to the nations, Israel succumbed to the ways of the pagan nations. In fact, they didn't even live up to the standards of those they were supposed to be an example to.

☑ Apply

God will not allow his name to be disgraced by his wayward people. If Israel is a witness to God, then its behaviour brings him into disrepute. There can be no more terrible words for God to say than "I am against you" (5:8).

God set Jerusalem in the centre of the nations. Where has He placed you? Are you a light to those around you? Or have you succumbed to their ways?

I am the LORD!

Why does God come in judgment against his people? Why can't he just forgive and forget? Why does a loving God bring disaster?

Disaster has come
Read Ezekiel 7:1-11

> ❓ *What is the point of the judgment that is unleashed on God's people (v 4, 9)?*

The time is now. The day is here. The end has come. Israel's accumulating wickedness has reached the point when God's judgment is unleashed. God's mercy and kindness had left them untouched for so long that perhaps they, and those who looked on, thought that God was nothing, and did not care. Now they all know the truth of the matter.

It has come to all
Read Ezekiel 7:12-14

> ❓ *What did God's people believe would insulate them from disaster? Did it?*

But this is not just to God's people. No one will benefit from the coming disaster. All would be included. Wealth would be no protection.

> ❓ *What reasons does God give for his judgment falling (see v 4, 8-9, 13, 27)?*

God's wrath is not arbitrary—it comes in direct *response* to our sin and rebellion. God's wrath is not frenzied or uncontrolled—it is *proportionate* to our sin.

Then you will know
Read Ezekiel 6:1-14

> ❓ *What repeated phrase here shows why God is doing all this?*

Seven times in these two chapters God says that he acts so that "you will know that I am the Lord" (6:7, 10, 13 and 14; and 7:4, 9 and 27). Those who survive will realise that God's judgment was justified. They will realise that God is Lord and King. And his rule cannot be rejected without consequences. If God could so easily be dismissed and rejected, he would not be God. And this means that in at least one sense the judgment of God is good news.

⌃ Pray

"Hallowed be your name" (Matthew 6:9) is a prayer that's God's name will be honoured. In situations where you see God dismissed or rejected, pray "hallowed be your name".

Praise God that for those who trust in Christ, God has already come in judgment—on Christ—so that for us there is no condemnation.

Idols in the midst

Idolatry. Isn't that what primitive people do? Yet modern people are as idolatrous in their pursuit of pleasure and possessions as well as their ideological allegiances.

But could idolatry be even more insidious? Could there be idolatry among God's people? Could there be idolatry in your life and in your church?

Idolatry—then and now
Read Ezekiel 8:1-18

- ❷ *Where is Ezekiel taken in his vision?*
- ❷ *How should that have made him feel?*
- ❷ *What does he discover there instead?*

Tammuz was the Babylonian god of plant life whose "death" was mourned each year as the autumn leaves fell. In Jerusalem God shows Ezekiel the idolatry of the people. But this idolatry doesn't take place in pagan shrines or high places. No, this idolatry takes place in God's holy temple!

- ❷ *How does God view idolatry (v 17-18)?*

⏷ Apply

At the end of his first letter, John warns Christians to avoid idolatry (1 John 5:21). Is it possible that there is idolatry among God's people today? Could there be idolatry in your life? Consider the following questions:

- ❷ *Do we ever make material possessions more important than serving God?*
- ❷ *Does our desire for pleasure drive our approach to our worship and meetings?*
- ❷ *Do worldly notions of success affect our evaluation of Christian work?*
- ❷ *Do we have an expectation of entertainment in churches and conferences?*
- ❷ *Do our prayers reflect earthly priorities or heavenly priorities?*

The end of the line?
Read Ezekiel 9:1-11

- ❶ *What is God's response to the apostasy of his people (v 1-2, 5-7)?*
- ❷ *How does Ezekiel respond?*
- ❷ *What is God's answer? Why (v 10)?*
- ❷ *Will anyone be spared (v 3-4, 10)?*

Is this the end of the line for God's people and God's promises? It certainly looks that way. *Will anyone be left?* asks Ezekiel.

God's response to Ezekiel's question is to say that the sin of God's people is great. They have been unjust to one another and dismissed God. God's judgment is justified. None of us has a leg to stand on. We all deserve God's judgment. But even as God reminds Ezekiel that his judgment is justified, a man reports that he has completed his task. And what is that task? To mark out the few who are faithful to God and grieved by the nation's sin. A remnant will be spared. God's purposes will continue.

God in our midst

Ezekiel's visit to Jerusalem continues. Things are looking up as Ezekiel sees the glory of God in the temple of Jerusalem. But then events take the most tragic turn possible.

God with his people

Read Ezekiel 10:1-17

> ❓ *Try to imagine the scene, and to feel what Ezekiel must have been feeling.*
> ❓ *What thoughts and emotions spring to mind?*

Ezekiel sees again something of the vision of chapter 1—the glory of God in the temple of God. God is present with his people—it is the story of the Bible from the beginning.

- **Eden**—God's intention is to be with humankind. He walks with Adam and Eve in the garden. But when they sin they are driven from his presence
- **Sinai**—God comes near his people, but the glory is more than sinful people can bear. Moses goes up the clouded mountain alone.
- **The tabernacle and temple**—both symbolised the glorious presence of God with his people.

God leaves his people

Read Ezekiel 10:18-22

> ❓ *What terrible thing happens (v 18-19)?*

This is one of the most poignant moments of Ezekiel's ministry. The greatest tragedy possible befalls God's people—God's glory departs from the temple. God is no longer present with his people. And nobody seems to notice. The closing words of the chapter picture the resolute faces of the cherubim as they march away from Jerusalem, with the glory of God going with them.

···· TIME OUT ····································

Read Exodus 33:15-21

Moses knew that there was no point in being saved from Egypt only to be left to live without God's presence.

✓ Apply

If we sneak a look at the final chapter of Ezekiel we find a vision of a new temple in a renewed city, the name of which is "The LORD is there"—the last words of this book. But where do we look for its fulfilment? Jesus of course. John 1:14 says: "The Word became flesh and made his dwelling among us. We have seen his glory, the glory of the one and only Son, who came from the Father, full of grace and truth." Ezekiel's vision is fulfilled in the one who made His dwelling among us and in whom we see God's glory. Christ is the true temple and tabernacle of God. And his glory is seen most clearly in his death on the cross.

> ❓ *What does it mean for us now to say we can know God's presence?*
> ❓ *What will it mean in the future (see Revelation 21:3, 22)?*

The route to blessing

We're going to spend a few Sundays understanding and meditating on Psalm 1. It tackles a fundamental question for most people: how can I be happy?

Read Psalm 1

❓ *What is the first step towards being blessed by God (v 1)?*

❓ *Why is this message so unpopular with our world today?*

The message is "repent". Being blessed by God involves turning away from practices and attitudes that may be normal, enjoyable, and even seem "sensible" to us.

Beware walking with the "wicked"

❓ *What do you think it means to "walk in step with the wicked"?*

It is a mistake to think that "wicked" counsel is limited to those who might encourage us to lie, steal or harm others. In the Bible, wickedness refers to any way of living that leaves God out of the picture. Wicked counsel is both the encouragement of friends to waste money on frivolities, and the "sensible" advice of a kindly grandmother who tells you to "look after number one".

❓ *Can you think of some subtle (and so more dangerous) ways in which people might live by "wicked" counsel?*

Care in company

❓ *Why is the company we keep so important?*

The company we keep—the friends we choose to spend time with—is one of the most significant factors in how our character develops. Their attitudes and values rub off on us without us noticing. And so all too easily we can find ourselves adopting the life, or "way", of "sinners"—those who deny and defy God's rule in life.

Steer clear of mockery

❓ *Why can mocking others be so tempting to do or to watch?*

Mockery puts us in the position of feeling we are superior to others. That makes it soul acid that eats away at us, leaving us with a distorted view of ourselves and a sneering cynicism about others.

✓ Apply

Think about your values—how you think life should be lived. Think about the friends you spend time with, the comedy shows you watch, the books you read.

❓ *What effect do they have on you? Could they be leading you away from enjoying life under God's rule?*

❓ *Are there any practical steps you need to take?*

❓ *Is there anything you're trying to avoid confronting? Remember—without repentance, there is no blessed life!*

Hope: true and false

People everywhere are in denial. Many are convinced God won't come in judgment. Others think that if he does, they'll be ok. "On the whole I've lived a good life", they say, "I've never harmed anyone".

False hope
Read Ezekiel 11:1-13

> ❓ *What opinion do the leaders have of themselves?*
> ❓ *What is God's view of them?*

More news from Jerusalem (Ezekiel does not return to Babylon until 11:24). The leaders, Jaazaniah and Pelatiah, are reassuring the people. "We'll be ok. Things will soon be back to normal with people building houses. We're in the cooking pot, safe from the fire". But things are not ok. The people are safe in the cooking pot, but not for long.

> ❓ *How are Ezekiel's words confirmed (v 13)?*
> ❓ *What does Ezekiel ask as a result?*

True hope
Read Ezekiel 11:14-17

God destroys the false hope of the people. And so Ezekiel asks again (v 13) if this is the end. Is there no hope left?

> ❓ *What message does Ezekiel now convey to the people (v 16-17)?*
> ❓ *What is God's purpose in doing this?*

All human hope is at an end. But there is hope in God. God will gather his people. He will accomplish a new exodus—bringing his people from bondage into the place of blessing. Of course, God's people did return to the land, but the real fulfilment of this prophesy is found in 1 Peter 1:3-5.

True purpose
Read Ezekiel 11:18-25

> ❓ *How will this restored remnant be different? What will God do for them?*
> ❓ *What is God's purpose in this (v 18-19)?*

The restoration of God's people is not an end in itself. God's people had failed to be what God called them to be: a light to the nations. Now, with his Spirit within them, they are finally capable of rising to the task.

☑ Apply

> ❓ *How is this fulfilled (see 1 Peter 2:9-12)?*
> ❓ *Think about the phrase "an undivided heart" (Ezekiel 11:19). What does it mean for you to have an undivided heart?*

⌃ Pray

Talk to the Lord about your own struggles. Use Romans 7:21-25 to confess your divided heart to God, and ask him to give you a heart devoted to him.

False hope exposed

In chapters 12 – 13 Ezekiel continues the theme of false hope, dismissing the false sources of confidence.

❓ *What false hopes do people today have that make them think they won't be judged by God?*

Packing list
Read Ezekiel 12:1-20

❓ *What strange instruction does God give to Ezekiel?*
❓ *What is its meaning?*

Ezekiel acts out the fate of the people left in Jerusalem. The details are evocative of Israel's recent history. In 2 Kings 25:1-16 we read that Zedekiah and the people rebel against the invaders and so are besieged. Zedekiah and the army break through the wall (hence Ezekiel 12:5, 7 and 12), but are captured and exiled to Babylon. Zedekiah himself has his eyes put out (hence 12:13).

Is judgment delayed?
Read Ezekiel 12:21-28

❓ *What false hopes are the people clinging on to?*
❓ *What is God's crushing response to these false hopes (v 28)?*

"Judgment hasn't come and so won't come." "Judgment won't come for ages so let's not worry about it." These statements have a very modern ring about them. But there are other false hopes that they hold as well.

Peace in our time?
Read Ezekiel 13:1-16

❓ *Who is Ezekiel's message for?*
❓ *What are they saying?*
❓ *What will become of them*

Ezekiel preaches to preachers. The false prophets proclaim peace—and those are the preachers people want to listen to. But they are like cowboy builders who put up a flimsy structure and hope a coat of paint will make it ok. When the storms come it will be swept away. God will punish those who only listen to what they want to hear, by giving them what they want—false prophecies.

❓ *Who would you put in the "false prophet" category today?*

It's a kind of magic
Read Ezekiel 13:17-23

❓ *What effect do these charms have?*
❓ *How do the "righteous" respond (v 22)?*

Something of this superstitious attitude is all around us: "touch wood". How can we respond to horoscope readers and the like in a way which our belief in the power and sovereignty of God, and points them to the gospel.

❓ *And are there "superstitious" elements to the Christianity of people in your own church? And what about you?*

False hope explored

Yesterday we saw that Ezekiel exposes the false hope of the people. But he hasn't finished yet.

False hope in God
Read Ezekiel 14:1-11

> ❷ *What positive thing happens (v 1)?*
> ❷ *But what is really going on inside?*

Some people thought they would be ok because they sought God. Sounds good. But their lives were deeply compromised. They sought God, but they also worshipped idols—at least in their hearts.

False hope in goodness
Read Ezekiel 14:12-23

> ❷ *What are people putting their trust in?*
> ❷ *What is God's answer to this false hope?*
> ❷ *Who will be saved (v 22-23)?*

Noah, Daniel and Job were clearly men known for their righteousness. The Daniel—or "Danel"—mentioned here is probably not the Daniel of lions' den fame who was only a young man at the time (see the NIV footnote). Surely having the likes of Noah and Job around meant everything would be okay? But they cannot save other people (v 14, 16, 18 and 20). Only those who are faithful to God will be saved.

☑ Apply

Do you think you're okay with God because you are associated with godly people? Perhaps your parents are Christians (v 16).

Perhaps you belong to a good church. Ezekiel says that unless you yourself are right with God, it is false hope.

A useless vine
Read Ezekiel 15:1-8

> ❷ *What is the thrust of the illustration used here?*
> ❷ *With all their false hopes exposed, what is the verdict on God's people?*

Judgment. Israel is like a useless vine. The wood of the vine is too twisted to be of much use. How much more useless when it has been burnt! Yet this is useless Israel's fate. Israel is a useless vine.

☑ Apply

> ❷ *Who is the true vine (see John 15:1-8)?*

If you are feeling out of touch with God, then maybe it's worth asking whether there is some compromise in your life.

···**TIME OUT**···

Look back over Ezekiel 1 – 15. What view of God does it portray? Do you need to revise your understanding of God?

If you find all this talk of judgment wearing, reflect on why that might be. Could it be that your view of God is inadequate? Could it be that your view of sin is inadequate?

Wounded love

Chapter 16 is a chapter of pain and poignancy. It describes God as a lover wounded by the actions of a deeply unfaithful wife.

A faithless people

God gently and graciously cares for Israel—a illegitimate and abandoned child—making her beautiful. But Israel turns to sordid prostitution, which is not even prostitution for she pays her lovers. And God is heartbroken and outraged by her unfaithfulness. As you read it try to imagine the love and pain of God, perhaps by imagining how you would feel if your husband, wife or close friend rejected you.

Read Ezekiel 16:1-59

> ❷ *What were your dominant feelings as you read this allegorical story?*

A faithful God

Read Ezekiel 16:60-63

> ❷ *Despite all that has gone before, what is God still prepared to do?*

This is not the end. God will save his people. God will atone for his people—righting the wrong done against himself. Because of his covenant promises, he will make a new covenant with them. And, of course, this points to Jesus who makes a new covenant with his own atoning blood. This long painful chapter of the adultery of God's people has a point. God wants his people to remember their ways for a reason.

> ❷ *What is the reason (v 61)?*

And by the way...
Read Ezekiel 16:49-50 again

> ❷ *What was Sodom's sin? How is this different from what we usually think?*

We assume that the key sin of Sodom was homosexual practices (hence "sodomy"). But that crime was committed *after* God had already pronounced judgment (Genesis 18:20-21). Ezekiel says Sodom's key sin was something much closer to home for all of us.

> ❷ *How does this make you feel about your own sin and unfaithfulness to God?*
> ❷ *"Overfed and unconcerned".What would Ezekiel say to our churches today?*

☑ Apply
Read 1 Peter 1:18-19

> ❷ *What does the cross show us about our sin—how serious it is—and the cost of putting it right?*
> ❷ *Once again: How does this make you feel about your own sin and unfaithfulness to God?*

True security

When you think about the future, what gives you confidence? Your job? Your skills? Your savings? Your pension? Your contacts? How would you feel about giving them all up?

The story
Read Ezekiel 17:1-10

Ezekiel tells a dramatic and memorable parable.

> ❓ *The details are clear, but can you guess at the meaning, and the challenge?*

The meaning
Read Ezekiel 17:11-21

It seems the people do not understand so God explains the meaning—you can also read the details of the story in 2 Kings 25.

> ❓ *What was the great sin of Zedekiah (see Ezekiel 17:18)?*
> ❓ *What will happen to him as a result?*

⌄ Apply

In many ways, Zedekiah's alliance with Egypt seemed immensely sensible. With just a small army of his own against the invading hordes, he turned to Pharaoh who had a "mighty army and great horde" at his disposal (v 17). And yet it is Pharaoh who failed them. It's the same with us. Our jobs, skills, savings, children, connections, property and pensions all seem very real and solid when compared to a word of promise from an invisible God.

> ❓ *Who or what is your "Egypt"?*

Where true hope lies
Read Ezekiel 17:22-24

> ❓ *How does what God promises to do echo the first part of this chapter?*
> ❓ *But what is different?*
> ❓ *How is it guaranteed (v 24)?*

God is going to do what the Babylonians have done, but on a much grander scale. He's going to plant a shoot that will become "a splendid cedar" (v 23) dwarfing all other trees (v 24). In other words, God is going to take the remnant of his discredited people and fashion a kingdom that will one day fill the earth.

···· TIME OUT ·······································
Read Matthew 13:31-32

> ❓ *Do you see now what this parable means?*

⌃ Pray

Zedekiah put his trust in the horses and armies of Egypt instead of the promises of God.

Talk honestly to the Lord about where your trust lies. Ask for his help to grow your trust in his word of promise.

Make the words of Psalm 91:2 your own:

> *"I will say of the LORD, 'He is my refuge and my fortress, my God, in whom I trust'."*

Just and unjust deserts

All of us have said it—many of us repeatedly—and if you're a parent, you will have heard it constantly on the lips of your children. We're all quick to say: "It's not fair!"

It's not fair!

Read Ezekiel 18:1-2, 25-29

> ❓ *What are the people complaining about?*
> ❓ *Is there substance to their complaint, do you think?*

It's not fair, the people were saying. We're being punished for the sins of Manasseh (see 2 Kings 21:11-12). On the surface, it seems unfair that the children should be condemned for the sins of their parents. But, while God deals with Israel as a whole, we have already seen how he exempts from judgment those who are faithful to him.

Now God develops this further.

Personally accountable

Read Ezekiel 18:3-4, (5-18), 19-20

> ❓ *What big principles does God hold to?*
> ❓ *What case studies does he present to show the truth of what he is claiming?*

No one will die for the sins of someone else because we are personally responsible to God. He spells out what he means:

- A good father will escape the judgment on the nation (v 5-9).
- An evil son will not be saved by the goodness of his father (v 10-13).
- A good son will not be condemned by his father's sins (v 14-18).

The promise that we will only be judged

for our own sin is not much of a promise if we're all sinners! And so we get a fourth case study.

- A repentant sinner who turns to God will be saved despite *everything* and *anything* he has done (18:21-23).

The implication is clear. Personal accountability means there must be personal repentance.

Ezekiel 18 emphasises human responsibility. Other passages emphasise God's sovereignty with God taking the decisive initiative (e.g. Ephesians 1). The Bible refuses to affirm divine sovereignty or human responsibility in a way that denies the other.

I take no pleasure

Read Ezekiel 18:23, 30-32

What is the evidence that God takes no pleasure in the death of anyone? It is the gospel call to repentance. The gospel— God's costly provision for us to escape the coming judgment—is the evidence of God's concern for mankind. What evidence is there that you take no pleasure in anyone's death? The evidence that counts is that you make the gospel call to repentance to others.

⸱⸱⸱ TIME OUT ⸱⸱⸱⸱⸱⸱⸱⸱⸱⸱⸱⸱⸱⸱⸱⸱⸱⸱⸱⸱⸱⸱⸱⸱⸱⸱⸱⸱⸱⸱⸱⸱⸱⸱⸱⸱

Read Ezekiel 19

> ❓ *Do you lament over the lost like this?*

The way of blessing

The first step to blessing, as we saw last Sunday, is to repent. The second is to believe.

Delight

Read Psalm 1

❓ *What do you think it means to "delight ... in the law of the LORD" (v 2)?*

At first sight this may seem a little weird. Perhaps it conjures up an image of people who are obsessive about rules and take delight in pointing out how others break them. The worst caricature of a Christian, in fact. But that is to miss the point. The "law" refers to the OT books of the law—the first five books of our Bible—which are the story of God's dealings with mankind, and his choosing and blessing of the people of Israel. The "rules" of godly living (e.g. the Ten Commandments) are about our grateful and dutiful response to the God who saves us. And notice how personal it is: "his law" as well as "the law". It is the expression of the character and purposes of a personal God who relates to me personally.

···· TIME OUT ·································

Read Exodus 20:1-3

Verse 2 is key to understanding the commandments. They are not rules to live by to find the blessing of God. They are the way to please the God who has *already* blessed you.

···

✅ Apply

The first readers of this psalm would have delighted in the way God had rescued them from Egypt so they could live his way as his people. Now we are to delight in the gospel of Christ—at the way he has rescued us from sin and death, so we can enjoy living his way as his people for ever.

❓ *Think about what you take most delight in. How does the gospel compare?*
❓ *How can you delight more in who Jesus is, and in living for him?*

One answer to that is coming up now!

Meditate

❓ *What do you think it might mean to meditate on God's law "day and night"?*
❓ *How is that different from the person of verse 1?*

The gospel should be what drives us, not the advice of others or the way the world works, or even what *we* think. The gospel is what delivers to us the blessing of God— true happiness. It is the thing that we must come back to all the time when we are deciding what to think or how to live.

🔼 Pray

Talk to God about the gospel. Delight in him; delight in what he has done for you. And ask God to prompt you to think about the gospel constantly, day and night, so that it would remove any other influence that would rob you of your blessing.

A history lesson

What do you think of the law of God? Is it a bit of a pain? Something we put up with out of gratitude to God? An obstacle to evangelism perhaps?

The patterns of history
Read Ezekiel 20:1-29 (30-32)

> ❓ *What is the substance of Ezekiel's speech to the elders? What's the overall message?*
> ❓ *How is the law shown to be good (v 11)?*
> ❓ *What is the result of following alternatives (v 25-26)?*

Ezekiel the dramatist and storyteller now becomes Ezekiel the historian. And he demonstrates that there is a pattern to Israel's history.

- The people of Israel turn from God and so ought to be judged (v 8).
- Instead, for the sake of his reputation, God redeems them (v 9-10).
- God gives, or reminds them of, the law (especially the Sabbath) so that they might live under his life-giving rule (v 11-12).
- But the people turn from God and so the pattern repeats itself from one generation to the next (v 13-20, 21-26).

The rule of God
Read Ezekiel 20:33-34

> ❓ *Is this a promise or a threat?*
> ❓ *What is God's aim in all of this?*

The Lord is determined that the cycle will not continue indefinitely. God will rule his people. If they will not accept the life-giving rule of his word, then he will rule them with "outpoured wrath". If we reject the rule of God, then he will come like a conquering King and impose his rule in judgment.

God's law is a gift (v 12). God reigns through his word. And God's reign brings life (v 11) and the knowledge of God (v 20). The law is not the imposition of a tyrant. The word of God brings freedom and life. Indeed, God punishes the people by allowing them alternative standards that, in the end, will fill them with horror.

✓ Apply

> ❓ *How do you see similar principles working in society today?*
> ❓ *How can we share the gospel message with those who are living like this?*

The honour of God
Re-read Ezekiel 20:9-10,14, 22

> ❓ *Why does God keep on saving his rebellious people?*
> ❓ *For what purpose (see v 38)?*

⌃ Pray

Ask God to help you experience Psalm 19:7:

> *"The law of the LORD is perfect, refreshing the soul. The statutes of the LORD are trustworthy, making wise the simple."*

God rules the nations

God's people will be judged by fire and by the sword—pictures of the destruction about to be wreaked by Babylon. But Babylonian aggression is only a part of the picture.

The sword of God

Read Ezekiel 20:45 – 21:12 (21:13-17)

❷ *What did Ezekiel say would happen?*
❷ *What response is called for (21:12)?*
❷ *What did the people think of his message (20:49)?*

A divine sword of judgment is coming. It is the sword of Babylon. At one and the same time Ezekiel can describe it as the sword of Babylon and the sword of God. The Babylonian kingdom is the instrument of God's purposes—despite all its wickedness. Even human evil and self-aggrandisement can be used by God to fulfil his purposes.

The pathways of God

Read Ezekiel 21:18-24

❷ *What does God tell Ezekiel to do?*
❷ *What does it signify?*

Ezekiel (dramatist, storyteller, historian) is now to be a civil engineer, marking out roads and erecting road signs. At the fork in the road the king of Babylon will have to choose between destroying Ammon and destroying Jerusalem. He will consult all manner of talismans. But in fact, it is God who will determine his actions. "The lot is cast into the lap, but its every decision is from the LORD" (Proverbs 16:33).

Read Ezekiel 21:25-26

All sorts of people think they control history—politicians, media moguls, businessmen. But in the end, it is they who will all be brought low before the true King.

The rightful ruler

Read Ezekiel 21:27-32

❷ *The great rulers in this world think they are in charge. But to whom does the kingdom rightfully belong (v 27)?*

Ammon escapes this time, but its time is coming. It will suffer the same fate as Jerusalem. The one who rules over the nations holds them to account. Dictators, torturers, corrupt officials, businesses that exploit: none of them get away with it—not in the end.

◢ Pray

God rules the nations. He determines the outcomes of history. He brings good out of evil. The things that fill us with anxiety in the world—disease, dictators, disasters—are all tools in his hands to fulfil his purposes. With this in mind...

- pray for nations who are suffering.
- pray for people you know who are suffering.
- pray for genuine humility among political leaders in your country and throughout the world.

X-rated religion

There are some bits of the Bible you just don't hear about in Sunday school. When God expresses himself like this, we can be sure there is something vital to convey.

It's the sort of language you wouldn't get away with in church (sneak a look at Ezekiel 23:20 for example). But some things demand outrage—like Israel's sin, for example. *And ours.*

The case against us

Read Ezekiel 22:1-31

- ❓ *What is God appalled by?*
- ❓ *What is at the root of it all (v 12)?*
- ❓ *Who is implicated (v 25-29)?*

We are guilty of all kinds of sin, although at root they all express our failure to love God and to love one another (see v 4). But this is not the kind of failing that is limited to a few powerful people. All kinds of people are implicated—princes, priests, officials, prophets, everyone in fact (v 29). The evil is, as we would say today, systemic.

- ❓ *God has always loved his people and counted them as precious, but what does he think of them now (v 17-18)?*

The fact is we are like dross—the impure stuff that gets thrown away. But listing sins doesn't do justice to the outrage of our rejection of God. So Ezekiel tells another story...

Vile sisters

It's the story of two sisters, Oholah and Oholibah, who represent Samaria (the capital of the northern kingdom of Israel)

and Jerusalem (the capital of the southern kingdom of Judah). They start life as prostitutes in Egypt, but really they belong to God. Oholah goes lusting after Assyrians who strip her and kill her—just as Samaria was destroyed in the eighth century B.C. Instead of learning the lesson, Oholibah copies her sister. And so God will have her "lovers" publicly disgrace her.

Skim-read Ezekiel 23:1-49

- ❓ *How do you feel having read the story of Oholah and Oholibah?*
- ❓ *What does it show of how God views your sin?*
- ❓ *What is the point of the story—see verses 48-49?*

✔ Apply

- ❓ *We can view them as little indulgences, but what does God think of your sins?*
- ❓ *How can we capture a more serious view of sin in ourselves without descending into guilt-induced paralysis?*

▲ Pray

If we claim to be without sin, we deceive ourselves and the truth is not in us. If we confess our sins, he is faithful and just and will forgive us our sins and purify us from all unrighteousness. (1 John 1:8-9)

End of part one

Think for a moment about the things that give people hope for the future. Think about what gives you hope. For the people of Ezekiel's day it was the temple.

The problem was that the temple was about to be destroyed—and with it the hopes of the people, and the siege of Jerusalem was about to begin.

What's cooking?
Read Ezekiel 24:1-14

In chapter 11 the people cite a proverb—*As meat belongs in the cooking pot, so they will be safe in Jerusalem.* Now the picture changes. The people are like meat in a pot, but don't expect a delicious stew. The heat is on and Jerusalem will burn. The people thought they'd be safe in Jerusalem. After all, that's what Psalm 48 says. But they'd missed the point. It's not the strong walls of Jerusalem that gives safety—it's the presence of God. But what if God is against you? What's cooking? *You are.*

Beyond grief
Read Ezekiel 24:15-24

- ❓ *What shocking sign does God give to Ezekiel, and how must he respond?*
- ❓ *What will his actions—or lack of them—show to the people?*
- ❓ *What understanding is this meant to lead them to (v 24)?*

Before the end comes, God has one last, devastating prophetic act for Ezekiel—the death of his wife. Ezekiel's wife was clearly precious to him—God calls her "the delight of your eyes" (v 16). It is as if this is the final, climactic sign that Ezekiel can make to get through to his indifferent audience. Just as the delight of Ezekiel's eyes dies, so the temple—the delight of the nation (v 21)—will soon be destroyed.

And Ezekiel is not to grieve. The trauma of the fall of Jerusalem and the destruction of the temple is *so great* that none of the usual customs of mourning will seem relevant. Why? Because the fall of Jerusalem is the sign of God's judgment.

Coming soon
Read Ezekiel 24:25-27

Chapter 24 is the end of part one of Ezekiel. Ezekiel has nothing to say to Judah now until the message of the fall of Jerusalem comes (as it does in 33:21). Ezekiel has systematically destroyed the false hope of Judah. When God is against you there can be no hope. But when the message does come, Ezekiel begins to proclaim good news. There is still hope—hope in what God will do.

Pray

Pray for those going through bitter suffering at the moment. Ask that the Lord would open their hearts to see his hand at work.

The God of all nations

For 24 chapters Ezekiel has been passing judgment on Israel. But so what? We're not part of Israel. We can look on with smug condescension. Or can we?

In chapters 25 – 32 Ezekiel turns his attention to the surrounding nations, moving anti-clockwise around Israel. Some of the nations were saying, "Great. This is our opportunity. Serves them right". Others were saying, "Israel is no different to us. Israel's God is no different to our gods. In fact, our gods are greater because Israel is in disarray". Ezekiel responds...

Do not delight
Read Ezekiel 25:1-7 (8-11)

> ❓ *What is promised and why?*
> ❓ *What is the point (v 7)?*

Again and again God says to the nations, *I am against you*—just as he said to Israel in chapters 1 – 24. God's judgment against sin is a universal reality. Israel's defeat and exile is a picture of the reality faced by all people in every nation.

Beware
Read Ezekiel 25:12-17

> ❓ *Why does God judge (v 7, 17)?*

Again and again God says to the nations, "You will know that I am the LORD"—just as he said to Israel in chapters 1 – 24. God meets with Ezekiel in Babylon and sits on a throne which is mobile (see chapter 1). Israel failed to be a light to the nations, but instead publicly profaned God's

name. So God acts to reveal himself to the nations. So the message to the nations is the same as the message to Israel. *You will know that God is the LORD. And this Lord is against you because of your sin.* God is Lord of all nations. And when God is against you, your only hope is in God himself.

TIME OUT
Read 1 Timothy 3:16

Part of the definition of the Christian message is that Israel's God is God of all nations— that our God is God of all nations. And so Christ must be preached to all nations.

> ❓ *Do you share God's vision for the peoples of the world?*
> ❓ *How is this expressed in your thinking and actions day by day?*

⌃ Pray

Is the gospel mission to the world part of your daily prayer routine? Consider using something like Operation World (OM Publishing) to pray day by day for the peoples of the world.

Tyre and Egypt

Ezekiel singles out two nations for special attention—Tyre and Egypt. Each receives a general prophecy of judgment, a lament, and a denouncement of their leader.

We're only going to dip into sample readings from these long chapters today. If you have time, read the section in brackets.

Pride and exploitation
Read Ezekiel 28:1-19 (26:1 – 28:26)

Ezekiel announces the fall of Tyre—the greatest trading nation of its day. Once the trade of Tyre had been good. It had provided materials for Solomon's temple (1 Kings 5) and "satisfied many nations" (Ezekiel 27:33).

Read 29:1-5 (29:1 – 32:32)

Ezekiel announces the destruction of Egypt—once the greatest military nation. But now Tyre and Egypt will be judged. Both will soon be overwhelmed by Babylon's armies.

> ❷ *Why are these two mighty nations to be judged (28:2, 17, 18, 29:6-7)?*

Fall and rise

Isaiah also speaks of Tyre's destruction (see Isaiah 23), but goes on to speak of her restoration. Once again she will "ply her trade with all the kingdoms on the face of the earth" (v 17). But this time "her profit and her earnings will be set apart for the LORD". Isaiah looks forward to the rebuilding of the temple when Tyre again will provide materials (Ezra 3:7). But he looks beyond this, too, to the day when the trading wealth of the nations will be used not for selfish, proud human ends but for the glory of God and the provision of his people (Isaiah 60:5 and Revelation 21:24-26).

☑ Apply

> ❷ *Does your trade or work glorify God and bless other people? Or is it an expression of pride and oppressive of others?*
> ❷ *What responsibilities do we have as Christians to call out the pride and exploitation of people and resources by companies?*

Singled out

> ❷ *Why are Tyre and Egypt singled out, do you think?*

Israel looked to Tyre for economic security and to Egypt for military security (see Ezekiel 29:16). But they should have looked to God. These chapters are designed to be overheard by God's people. They are a reminder that God is Lord of every nation in the world, and that the ultimate confidence of his people should be in him.

> ❷ *How do you stack up in that regard?*

Talk to the Lord about your answer.

The mark of the blessed

How do you spot someone who is truly blessed by God?

❓ *What is the quality you most look for in friends, work colleagues or others?*

There may be many things—good humour, professionalism, truthfulness. Did you have words like faithfulness and reliability somewhere on your list? Whatever their character, if an acquaintance is faithful and not flighty, constant not capricious, then they are someone you can trust and depend on.

Read Psalm 1:3

Think about the image of a tree being used here.

❓ *Why is the tree "evergreen", do you think?*

❓ *What are the visible results of its invisible source of nourishment?*

A Christian shows constancy, or stickability, because they have built their life on Christ, who is the same yesterday, today and for ever (Hebrews 13:8). As our spiritual life grows in us by the Holy Spirit's work in our hearts, we start to show the same qualities in our lives as Jesus did in his. We are not blown about by popular or clever-sounding opinions. We are not dragged off course by friends or enemies. We do not seek to feel better about ourselves, or gain recognition for ourselves, by pushing others down.

···· **TIME OUT** ··

Is the end of Psalm 1:3 a promise that Christians close to God will grow rich? Yes—and no! In the Old Testament God illustrated

with worldly wealth the blessing he poured out on those he loved. But this is an illustration only. Some believers will enjoy the blessing and responsibility of worldly wealth. Others will enjoy the blessing and responsibility of worldly poverty. We are all rich beyond our wildest dreams in Christ.

Read Ephesians 2:7 and 3:8

⌄ Apply

Is Psalm 1:3 a picture of the person you want to be? The clues to how to get there are in the image. Plant yourself in Christ. Draw your strength and sustenance from him. Meditate day and night on the gospel of God, and you will grow more like Christ by the grace and power of God.

❓ *As you look forward to the next week, at what time do you think you will be in most danger of forgetting about the gospel? What will you do at that point to remind yourself?*

⌃ Pray

Speak to God about verse 3 now. Ask him to establish you in Christ so that you will be evergreen, fruitful and wealthy in the only way that matters; and so that you will be a blessing to others.

Saying and listening

At the start of part two of Ezekiel we get a reminder of two key themes from the first half of the book.

Preacher's responsibility

Read Ezekiel 33:1-9

> ❓ *How would you summarise the point being made here?*

If a watchman sounds the warning, the people are responsible for their own fate. If the watchman does not sound the warning, the watchman shares responsibility for the fate of the people. In the same way, if Ezekiel does not warn of God's judgment, he shares responsibility for the fate of the people. But if he does warn, the people will be responsible for their own fate.

Hearer's responsibility

Read Ezekiel 33:10-16

It seems that the people recognised their sin was the problem. And yet they were not turning from it to God—what the Bible calls "repentance".

Objections

Read Ezekiel 33:17-20

> ❓ *What typical objections do people raise to Ezekiel's message of repentance?*
> ❓ *Have you heard people say similar things today?*
> ❓ *When people say these things, what are they showing about themselves?*
> ❓ *What is God's stark answer to them?*

But that's not fair, the people say. *What about all my good works? What about all the evil done by that other person?* But God is just. He will judge *everyone* according to what they have done. But what counts is repentance—not former good works, nor former wickedness. People cling on to these ideas because they do not accept the true reality of their own sinfulness, and that God will judge them for it. We love to compare ourselves with each other, and not with God himself.

⌄ Apply

Like Ezekiel, we too have a message to share with others—the gospel.

> ❓ *How does this passage encourage you to take this responsibility seriously?*

⌃ Pray

Identify before God one thing you could do to fulfil your responsibility to make the gospel known. Ask God to help you do it—today!

> ❓ *How real and deep is your repentance from the sin that you know God hates?*
> ❓ *Do you "manage" your repentance so that it just looks to others that you are living the Christian life, while secretly you are motivated by pride and self-reliance?*

Deaf ears

This is a key moment in Israel's history and Ezekiel's ministry. He has said there is no hope—God's people will be judged. And now judgment has come.

Prophesy confirmed
Read Ezekiel 33:21-22

Just as he predicted back in chapter 24, Jerusalem has fallen. The refugee arrives with the news, and Ezekiel can open his mouth once again. Now at last, the false hopes of the people are finally demolished. Ezekiel now speaks of the hope that God himself brings. But perhaps there is more "false-hope demolition work" to be done?

For or against you?
Read Ezekiel 33:23-29

❓ *Has the people's attitude changed now that disaster has come upon them?*

You would have thought the defeat of Jerusalem would have finally put an end to the false hopes of the people. But the people remain confident even though they are now dispossessed refugees. *Even if only a few of us remain,* they argue, *we are more than Abraham and he possessed the land.* But they've missed the point. Abraham possessed the land through the promise and power of God. But now God is against his people. What counts is not numbers, but whether God is for you or against you.

"Lovely sermon vicar"
Read Ezekiel 33:30-33

People liked listening to Ezekiel. He was a phenomenon; an interesting eccentric; an eloquent speaker. *But they did nothing about it.* Hearing God's word had become simply an amusing pastime. But Ezekiel's hearers won't be able to listen for ever. One day the desolation of which he speaks will come. Hearing God's word is not for entertainment or an amusing hobby, but an urgent call to action.

❓ *Think about your favourite preachers. Why do you like listening to them? Is it their "beautiful voice" (v 32), the entertainment factor? Or is there something else?*

❓ *What are the dangers of valuing eloquence and entertainment over content and Bible teaching?*

☑ Apply
Read James 1:22-25

❓ *What does James say about those who hear God's word, but don't practise it?*

❓ *What practical steps can you take to ensure you don't fall into this trap?*

Here are some suggestions.

- Memorise verses of the Bible—put them up in the kitchen.
- Keep a journal of your Bible learning and how it has changed you.
- Take notes during public teaching and identify action points.
- Find someone to share regularly what you have learnt and what you will do.

Fleeced!

Opinion polls show that our respect for, and trust in, leaders is declining. Are we more cynical? Does our individualistic age mistrust authority? Or have we simply been let down too many times?

Good and bad leaders

Where will we find good leadership? Not among Israel's leaders, it seems.

Read Ezekiel 34:1-10

> ❓ *Why is the shepherd/sheep metaphor that Ezekiel uses so appropriate (hint: think back to what David wrote)?*
> ❓ *How have they failed?*

They should have been like shepherds to God's people—caring for them and guiding them, as God, *their* shepherd does for them (Psalm 23). But instead, they have exploited and abandoned them. They have ruled "harshly and brutally" (Ezekiel 34:4).

> ❓ *What is God's verdict on the unfaithful shepherds of Israel?*

God will hold leaders accountable for what happens to those under their care (v 10).

I will tend my sheep

Read Ezekiel 34:11-22

> ❓ *Where will we find good leadership?*

God himself promises to search for and rescue his sheep. God himself promises to tend and restore them. God's rule means rescue and provision. Notice how God keeps saying, "I myself will... I will..." And look at what God promises to do. "I will... search for them... look after them... rescue them... bring them... pasture them... tend them...

make them lie down... and destroy and judge."

But God's rule also means justice and equity. God will not allow the strong to take advantage of the weak (v 16-22). With the talk of caring and tending comes a commitment to judgment and justice.

> ❓ *How does this description of God's rule redefine what it means for leaders to lead and rule?*
> ❓ *If you are in leadership—in the home, the church or the workplace—ask God to help you. You will be held accountable for those under your care.*

🔼 Pray

God's people can say with David, "The Lord is my shepherd". Read verses 11-16 and where it says "my sheep" or "them", read your own name.

The Shepherd-King

At the start of this chapter we saw that God's people were "harassed and helpless, like sheep without a shepherd". Sound familiar?

Read Matthew 9:36

It's not a coincidence. When Matthew wrote this verse he almost certainly had Ezekiel 34 in mind.

The coming of the king

Read Ezekiel 34:23-24

> ❷ *What wonderful promises are there in these verses?*
> ❷ *What is the guarantee it will happen?*

When things are bad, people often remember the great heroes of the past. "If only we had a king like David again". But these verses are not mere nostalgia. In fact, Ezekiel does not really look back at all. He is looking forward. David, the shepherd turned king, was Israel's greatest leader. Now God promises a new king like David, but greater than David. This new David will rule on God's behalf and tend his people. Matthew knew this promise was fulfilled in Jesus.

The rule of the king

Read Ezekiel 34:25-31

> ❷ *What will God do for his people?*
> ❷ *What is life like under his rule?*
> ❷ *What will this show (v 30-31)?*

Satan's lie in the Garden of Eden was to claim that the rule of God was oppressive. And ever since, we have thought ruling is about exercising power and control. We have made harsh and brutal rule (34:4) the norm.

But Jesus, the Shepherd-King, turns all those notions upside down when he lays down his life for his sheep. God's rule brings life and blessing; it brings peace and freedom.

⌄ Apply

In 34:11-16 God emphasises that he himself is going to shepherd his people. And then in verses 23-24 he promises to get David's Son to do it for him. These promises come together as the Son of God, great David's greater son, comes into the world and declares "I am the good shepherd. The good shepherd lays down his life for the sheep" (John 10:11).

Work through each of the blessings described in Ezekiel 34:25-31.

> ❷ *How are they fulfilled in the reign of the Good Shepherd?*
> ❷ *How is Jesus different from Israel's shepherds (v 2-6)?*

⌃ Pray

Give thanks to God for Jesus, the Good Shepherd.

Global warning

*"Blessed are the meek for they shall inherit the earth" said Jesus. It is a nice thought—
but isn't the reality that the pushy, the strong and the aggressive take possession?*

Judgment on Edom

Read Ezekiel 35:1-15

❓ *What two sins has Edom committed?*

Mount Seir was the greatest mountain
in Edom. In this passage it stands for the
nation as a whole. (The people of Israel
were descended from Jacob. The people of
Edom were descended from Esau—Jacob's
estranged brother. Hence the "ancient hostility" in v 5.) Ezekiel identifies two sins that
Edom had committed.

- **Treachery towards God's people (v 5, 10).**
  Edom will be judged because it exploited
  Israel's defeat.

- **Blasphemy towards God (v 13).** Edom
  thought the defeat of Israel meant the defeat of God. In reality, Israel's defeat was
  the vindication of God's holy name.

Edom's judgment will perfectly fit its crime
(v 11). Its sin will rebound on itself. Because
it rejoiced in Israel's defeat, it will miss out
on the blessings of Israel's restoration
(v 14-15).

But haven't we been here before? See
25:12-14. This passage seems to be in the
wrong place. Shouldn't it be back in Ezekiel's address to the nations in chapters
25 – 32? No! It belongs alongside chapter
36...

Blessing on Israel

Read Ezekiel 36:1-12

❓ *What will God do for his people?*
❓ *What does God say to the land?*

The nations around Israel, especially Edom,
tried to rob it of the possession that God had
given to it. The exile to Babylon was God's
judgment against Israel. But his promise
to give Israel the land as its possession still
stood. If Edom was going to take possession
of the land it would run into conflict with
God's promise. Either Edom would fail or
God's promise would fail. No contest. In
the end Jesus is right: *it will be the meek who
inherit the earth.*

When God addresses the land he says that
not only will he ensure the land is Israel's
possession, he will also once again make it a
land of milk and honey; a land of prosperity
and blessing.

···· TIME OUT ····

Read Romans 8:19-22

❓ *How will creation share in salvation?*

☑ Apply

The land of Israel was only a picture of what
God plans for his people—a new heaven
and a new earth (see 1 Peter 1:3-5).

❓ *How secure is our inheritance with
God? Can anyone take it away?*

My great name

"Hallowed be your name", we pray in the Lord's Prayer. Throughout the book of Ezekiel God has acted to establish the honour of his name.

"Then they will know that I am the LORD" has been Ezekiel's refrain.

Dishonouring God

Read Ezekiel 36:13-23

God's people lived wicked lives and so God's holy name was brought into disrepute. God's people were supposed to live under his rule, according to his law in such a way that their neighbours and visitors recognised the goodness of God. Instead, the nations said, *If that is what his people are like, then what kind of God is their God.*

And so God judges his people to demonstrate that he is not like his wayward children. Unlike other "gods" of the ancient world, the LORD will not tolerate evil or accommodate disobedience. And yet they are still his people—the sheep of his pasture.

> ❷ *But what do the onlookers now say (v 20-21)?*
> ❷ *And so what will God do (v 22-23)?*

Now the nations will say, *God cannot care for his people. He cannot fulfil His promise.* And so God acts in salvation for the sake of his holy name; to vindicate his reputation.

So it is today. God will be glorified in the judgment of the wicked. He will re-establish his rule in the face of their rebellion. And God saves us to glorify his name and display his grace—not because of any worth in us. We have no hope because God must

be God. We cannot flout his rule for ever because, as God, he must rule. And yet at the same time, we can have hope because God will be God—he will keep his promises and he will show mercy.

☑ Apply

Today the most that many people know about Christ is what they learn from the lives of those who bear his name: Christ-ians.

> ❷ *What do people learn about Jesus from your life?*

---- **TIME OUT** ----

Read 1 Peter 1:15-19

> ❷ *What does it mean for us to know a holy God?*
> ❷ *What did it take for the God who cannot accommodate disobedience to know disobedient people?*

☒ Pray

Make the grace and glory of God the heart of your prayers and thanksgiving today.

Wages of wickedness

In the second half of this song, we are introduced to another great theme of the psalms: the ruin of those who reject God.

Incredible disappearance

Read Psalm 1

The signs of the person blessed by God are growth, endurance and fruitfulness (v 3).

> ❓ *What is the only reality about the wicked that really matters, according to verse 4?*

The wicked have no future. Like an insignificant by-product from a factory that's simply dumped. Or like the husks from the wheat, which are just an annoyance to the farmer. In the end their lives count for nothing; the wind blows and they are gone.

···· TIME OUT ·······

> ❓ *Do you struggle to believe that this is truly the way of things?*

The wicked dominate the news headlines every day. They seem so big, so permanent, so important and influential. By contrast, the humble, struggling believer seems so insignificant. But the eye of faith sees that, in God's value system, the opposite is true. It is sometimes hard to believe this—but it's something the writers of the psalms recognise and continually remind us of.

Read Psalm 73:1-20

Terrifying judgment

The blessed man looks to a new day coming when God's judgment will make the distinction clear for all to see. There will be no reprieve for the wicked on that day. No last-minute second chance. No place among God's people for those who have spent their lives mocking God's gospel.

> ❓ *Is this how you see your non-Christian friends and family? Even the "nice" ones?*

It's very easy to deceive ourselves on this issue. Our family, our closest mates, our beloved spouse even—all are facing the wrath of God's holy judgment, if they have chosen to defy him.

☑ Apply

Think about those people now.

> ❓ *How are you showing them what it is like to enjoy the blessing of life under God's rule?*
> ❓ *How, and when, might you be able to speak to them about how they might be blessed, and not blown away?*

God, who must judge, sent his Son to take that judgment. Ask him to work in the hearts of those you love but who don't love God, so that they won't have to endure his anger, but can enjoy his blessing.

A new people

A renewed land. A renewed kingdom. But how can it last unless there is a renewed people? How can we know God unless he wipes away the past and makes us new?

A new people
Read Ezekiel 36:24-30

> ❓ *How might a Jewish exile have heard these words as originally given?*
>
> ❓ *What added dimension comes from knowing they are fulfilled in Christ?*

- **I will gather you...** (v 24) "I have other sheep that are not of this sheep pen. I must bring them also. They too will listen to my voice, and there shall be one flock and one shepherd" (John 10:16).

- **I will cleanse you...** (Ezekiel 36:25) "But you were washed, you were sanctified, you were justified in the name of the Lord Jesus Christ and by the Spirit of our God" (1 Corinthians 6:11).

- **I will give you a new heart and a new spirit...** (Ezekiel 36:26) "Therefore, if anyone is in Christ, he is a new creation; the old has gone, the new has come!" (2 Corinthians 5:17).

- **I will put my Spirit in you...** (Ezekiel 36:27) "He redeemed us ... so that by faith we might receive the promise of the Spirit" (Galatians 3:14).

- **You will live in the land...** (Ezekiel 36:28-30) "But in keeping with his promise we are looking forward to a new heaven and a new earth, where righteousness dwells" (2 Peter 3:13).

A new resolve
Read Ezekiel 36:31-32

What happens when God renews his people? They remember their old ways with shame. And they have a new God-given commitment to following his word (v 27).

A new Eden
Read Ezekiel 36:33-36

The renewal of God's people goes hand in hand with the renewal of creation. God promises a new Eden. Just as mankind's sin infected creation (Genesis 3:17-19), so mankind's redemption leads to the renewal of creation.

A new community
Read Ezekiel 36:37-38

God promised Abraham that his offspring would be as numerous as the sand on the shore and the stars in the sky. Now he promises that the new people of God will be as numerous as a vast flock of sheep. And in Revelation John sees in heaven "a great multitude that no one could count" (Revelation 7:9).

> ❓ *How should this picture of gospel success affect our attitude towards mission and evangelism?*

Word and Spirit

As far as God is concerned, Israel is spiritually dead. In fact it is not even a warm corpse: just dry bones—long since dead. What hope can there be of resuscitation?

Note that this passage is not about individual life after death—although, of course, both the Old and New Testaments teach that. Instead, it is about the spiritual deadness of God's people as a whole.

Life through the word
Read Ezekiel 37:1-8

> ❷ *What impossible task does God give to Ezekiel?*
> ❷ *How does he respond?*
> ❷ *What is still missing?*

Ezekiel is to proclaim God's life-giving word to the valley of dry bones. And in response to God's word, an amazing transformation takes place. But it is not enough...

Life through the Spirit
Read Ezekiel 37:9-10

> ❷ *What is the relationship between the word of God and the Spirit (breath) of God?*

In the Hebrew language the word for "spirit" and "breath" are the same. The life-giving Spirit of God that brought dust to life at creation (see Genesis 2:7), now brings life to the corpses in the valley. Israel may be dead, cut off from God and without hope, but through God's word and his Spirit they can receive new life and new hope.

The word of God and the Spirit of God work together in the Bible. In creation, the word of God comes on the breath of God, creating where there was nothing, bringing order to chaos, giving life to lifeless beings. And in salvation, the Spirit gives life through the word; the Spirit renews the heart so that it responds in faith to the word.

True hope
Read Ezekiel 37:11-14

"Our hope is gone" (v 11). That was the message of Ezekiel 1 – 24. When God is against you there can be no hope—except in God himself. And now God speaks words of hope—true hope. He is going to bring life to dead Israel. He is going to bring back exiled Israel. Then they will know that he is the Lord.

⌄ Apply

Today people have all sorts of false hopes— false routes to happiness, false promises of fulfilment, false reassurance for death. There is no hope when God is against you. But in Christ, God is *for* us. And in Christ lies our true hope, our *only* hope.

And we must never separate the work of the Spirit from the power of God's word. They are inextricably intertwined—it is the way God works in bringing new life, refreshment and vitality to his people.

One nation under God

God's plan of salvation was never to save individuals on their own. His plan was to save a new people who would know him and be his people.

As Ezekiel speaks of salvation he reminds them of the goal of God's covenant—that they will be God's people and that God will be their God (see Ezekiel 34:31; 36:28 and 37:27).

One nation
Read Ezekiel 37:15-23

> ❓ *What visual aid is Ezekiel to make?*
> ❓ *What does it signify?*

But God's plan of salvation was not only to reconcile a people to himself. His plan was also to reconcile his people to one another. Ezekiel joins two sticks together to symbolise the reconciliation of the divided kingdom of Israel. During the reign of Rehoboam, Solomon's son, the kingdom had divided into two. One kingdom— Israel or Ephraim—was lost after exile into Assyria. The other—Judah—is currently exiled in Babylon. But one day, says Ezekiel, they will be gathered from exile and reunited.

Apply

But Ezekiel only saw half the picture.

Read Ephesians 2:11-18

God's intention is not only to gather together Israel. God's plan is to gather people from all nations. God's plan is to reconcile Jew and Gentile—the whole world—to himself through Christ.

One king
Read Ezekiel 37:22, 24-28

> ❓ *What does God promise his renewed people here?*

Ezekiel promises a new Shepherd-King like David. God will fulfil his promise to David—his son will reign forever (v 25). Under his rule God's people will: live in God's promised land (v 25); enjoy God's peace (v 26); and know God's presence (v 26-27).

These promises are fulfilled in Jesus, God's anointed Shepherd-King. In Christ, we have an inheritance in the new creation. In Christ, we have peace with God and reconciliation with one another. In Christ, God is with us—he walked among us and now lives with his people by his Spirit.

Apply
Read Ezekiel 37:28 again

When outsiders see God living among his reconciled people, they will acknowledge him as Lord. Paul says that God's wisdom is made manifest through the reconciliation of Jew and Gentile (Ephesians 3:6, 10). Jesus says that when people see our love and unity they will acknowledge that he is from God (John 13:34-35; 17:23).

> ❓ *How can we make our love for one another more visible to others?*

Trouble ahead?

Have you ever felt the pressure to keep quiet about your faith? Have you ever faced hostility because of Christ?

Thankfully, what most of us experience is mild compared to the persecution endured by many Christians. But hostility and opposition are part of the common experience of God's people. Ezekiel knew that.

All agog
Read Ezekiel 38:1-6

God declares that he is against Gog from the land of Magog because of his hostility to God's people. But who on earth is Gog and where is Magog? They can't be identified with any persons or places of Ezekiel's time. It's unlikely that they represent Babylon, as Ezekiel has been speaking of the return from Babylonian exile (see v 8). In fact all the names in these verses are drawn from what was, even for Ezekiel, ancient history.

Read Genesis 10:1-6

We should probably see these characters as timeless, symbolic figures. They were the descendants of two of Noah's sons, Japheth and Ham. Magog, Meshek, Tubal, Gomer and Togarmah were descendants of Japheth. They are joined by Cush, Egypt, Put and Canaan, the sons of Ham (Genesis 10:6). The Israelites were descended from Noah's third son, Shem. In other words, these figures represent all those throughout history who are not God's people and who oppose God's people. Many years later, the apostle John would speak of Gog and Magog gathering for battle against God's people (see Revelation 20:7-8).

Gog against God
Read Ezekiel 38:7-16

> ❓ *What does the army do and why, and why does God allow it?*

The army of Gog will come against God's people, "advancing like a storm". There is no neutrality in this battle.

⌄ Apply

> ❓ *Are you surprised when people are hostile to Christianity?*

Reflect on Jesus' words: "Whoever is not with me is against me" (Luke 11:23). We shouldn't be surprised at hostility. Jesus said: "In this world you will have trouble" (John 16:33).

God against Gog
Read Ezekiel 38:17-23

The ancient conflict between the kingdom of God and the kingdom of this world will come to a terrible, apocalyptic climax. God will come against Gog, just as Gog came against God's people. By coming against sin, God will demonstrate his holiness. By defeating those who defy him, God will demonstrate the greatness of his rule.

Pray today for persecuted Christians. Focus especially on situations known to you, and try to be specific.

Bible in a year: Psalm 119:88-176 • 2 Corinthians 5 ⌄

The victory of God

Let's be honest, this is how things often look: Jesus is not Lord. Or he doesn't care about evil. Power belongs to the devil, or at least to military dictators, media empires and multinationals. It certainly doesn't belong to the church. Right?

In chapter 38 we saw that Gog represents all those throughout history who are not God's people and who oppose God's people. But God is going to come against Gog.

A victory for God

Read Ezekiel 39:1-20

> ❷ *What is the outcome of this great battle?*
> ❷ *How complete is it?*

- This victory is so comprehensive that the discarded weapons of the enemy will provide firewood for seven years (v 9-10).

- This victory is so comprehensive that the burial mound of fallen enemy soldiers will block the way for travellers (v 11).

- This victory is so comprehensive that burying the dead and cleaning up afterwards will take seven months (v 12-16).

- This victory is so comprehensive that every bird and animal will feast on the fallen (v 17-20).

We see mirrored here the ultimate victory of Christ over sin, death and evil. Jesus has received all authority and he will be Lord of all. God will judge evil. He will defeat Satan and all who oppose his people.

A revelation to the world

Read Ezekiel 39:21-29

The word "apocalypse" means "revelation".

The final day will reveal to everyone what's really been going on and what God is really like.

People today may think God is of little consequence; they may think they are lords of their own destinies. But one day God will display his glory and authority to every nation on earth. People today may think that sin is of little consequence; they may scorn the weakness of the church. But one day God will vindicate his holiness and save his people.

☑ Apply

> ❷ *As Ezekiel's hearers came to terms with defeat and exile, how would the story of Gog encourage them?*
> ❷ *How would it encourage the persecuted Christians you prayed for yesterday? Pray that they will know that encouragement.*

◹ Pray

The final revelation is not just to the nations. God's people will see the extent of His holiness and sovereignty; they will know that he is LORD.

> ❷ *What surprises might await us on that day?*

Talk to God about your answer.

Planning a new temple

What do you think heaven will be like? A vast praise meeting? An endless cricket match? Rolling countryside? Or relaxing in a warm jacuzzi?

For Ezekiel it was a dream of a new temple.

A new temple
Read Ezekiel 40:1-9 (40:10 – 42:20)

❓ *What is Ezekiel shown?*

The description goes on for three chapters—scan the pages to see what it contains.

❓ *Does this description interest you?*
❓ *Why might it be of such great importance to Ezekiel and his hearers?*

Ezekiel has a tour guide to show him round. In great detail he is shown the outer courts and gates, the rooms for preparing sacrifices and the temple itself. The descriptions seem pretty boring to us, but Ezekiel started life as a priest in the temple. He notes down carefully the day he saw this (40:1). He is told to pay careful attention (v 4). For some reason this really matters.

When the Babylonians defeated Jerusalem, they destroyed the temple and carried away its treasures. The destruction of the temple epitomised the national disaster that had come upon Israel. The temple was the great symbol of God's presence with his people. A destroyed temple symbolised God abandoning his people in judgment.

God with us
Read Ezekiel 43:1-5

In Ezekiel 10 God's glory left the old temple.

Now there is a new temple filled with God's glory. God's judgment is satisfied. The awesome, holy God that Ezekiel glimpsed in his great vision (chapter 1) is once again present with his people (43:3). It is a thrilling message for God's people in exile.

But when was Ezekiel's vision fulfilled? It wasn't when Ezra brought the exiles back from Babylon and rebuilt the temple, but much, much later.

⌄ Apply
Read John 2:18-22

The temple was the symbol of God's presence. In Jesus, the reality has come. Like the old temple, he will be destroyed, but unlike the old temple, he was raised again in three days.

Read Mark 15:38

Through his death and resurrection, Jesus unites us with God. The old barriers between God and mankind are torn apart. We can know God and be with Him. However you imagine heaven, the key thing about it is the presence of God with His people

⌃ Pray

Thank God that through Christ's death we can know him, approach him in prayer and one day will be with him for ever.

Whose side is God on?

Nations and leaders have often used religion to validate their own political claims. But it is quite clear whose side God really is on. And it's nothing to do with race or nationality.

Two ways to live

Read Psalm 1 and focus on verse 6

❓ *What is the contrast made in verse 6?*

❓ *What do you think it means for the LORD to "watch over" us?*

It is significant that the verse uses the personal name of God, Yahweh (usually written as LORD in our English translations). Those who reject God will ultimately wither and die. Those who love him are watched over by the God who has saved us and has committed himself to us in the promise of the gospel. **Read Hebrews 13:5.**

There are millions of choices before us:

- What to wear.
- Who to support.
- What job to do.
- Where to live.
- Who to marry; how to spend our money.
- Which friendships to cultivate.
- What books to read.

But there are only two ways to live. And we express which way we have chosen to live in the way we make each and all of these decisions in everyday life.

The God who watches

"God is watching you—from a distance" goes the song. But nothing could be further from the truth. This verse reveals to us that God is watching us in an intimate, detailed, caring way that is filled with love. It's a closeness that those who don't know him feel uncomfortable with. But those who have experienced his saving love welcome it, revel in it and rejoice about it.

If you have never memorised Psalm 1, why not have a go this week? Then you can sing it to yourself all day, every day.

⌄ Apply

❓ *How do you react to the thought of God's constant watching presence?*

❓ *When something in the next week goes wrong for you, how can you use this truth to calm and encourage yourself?*

❓ *What would you have thought or done differently last week if you'd really known God was watching?*

❓ *What will you do differently this week because you remember that he is watching you and watching over you?*

⌃ Pray

Read through the whole psalm once again. Let its view of life challenge yours. Let its concerns become yours. Let its promises be yours to hold on to.

Then pray through each verse, pausing to thank God for what you find there, and/or to ask God to help you live according to the truths you see.

The point of the detail

We once had a neighbour who complained about the noise our children were making. For weeks afterwards we went round shushing them up whenever she was in.

But what if God was your next door neighbour? How would you behave then?

The presence of God
Read Ezekiel 43:6-9

When God lived among his people—"with only a wall between" (v 8)— they defiled his holy name. With a new temple and the return of God's glory there can be a new start. If God lived next door, you would make sure you did nothing to displease him.

❓ *But what if God lived within you? What if he not only lived with you, but gave you the resources to live a new life? What if he himself had borne the consequences of your past misconduct?*
❓ *How then would you want to live?*

The faithfulness of God
Read Ezekiel 43:10-12

❓ *Why do you think Ezekiel goes into so much detail, especially since it seems so boring to us?*

The fact that a new temple had to be built reminded the people of their sin. After all, it was their sin that had led to the destruction of the old temple. They knew God had every right to abandon them. So God's grace and faithfulness towards them highlighted their unfaithfulness towards him. Each new

detail in Ezekiel's description reminded them of their sin but also of God's faithfulness.

⌄ Apply

❓ *How should people who have benefited from the grace and faithfulness of God behave?*
❓ *How, for example, should it affect our attitude towards...*
   • *people who let us down?*
   • *the use of our money and time?*
   • *the marginalised in our society?*

⌃ Pray
Read 1 Corinthians 6:19-20

Ask God to help you live a life worthy of someone who has God living within them.

Coming before God

Prayer. It's difficult yet it's easy. It's difficult because we often struggle against distractions, against laziness, against self-confidence. But it's also remarkably easy.

It's quicker than writing a letter. It's more reliable than sending an e-mail. We don't have to perform any rituals, pay any fees, or go to any special place. It wasn't always so easy to come before God.

The right sacrifice
Read Ezekiel 43:25-27; 45:18-25

❓ *What is both exciting and concerning about 43:27?*

"Then I will accept you". The temple was the symbol of God's presence with his people. The new temple symbolises God's presence restored. But sinful people cannot come into the presence of a holy God. And God cannot merely disregard sin—that would compromise his holiness. All sorts of detestable and idolatrous practices had been going on in the old temple (see 8:5-11). Before the activities of the temple could begin, sacrifice must be made to reconsecrate it. And from then on regular sacrifice had to be made for the sin of the people. (For the full detail read 43:13-27 and 45:13 – 46:24.)

The right priesthood
Read Ezekiel 44:15-16

A new temple meant a renewed priesthood. (For the full detail read 44:1-31.) Those who had been involved in the old corrupt ways could serve in the temple, but they were forbidden from offering sacrifices in God's presence (44:10-14). And even those who had remained faithful had to keep themselves pure (44:17-27).

What Ezekiel describes is new. It is not just a restoration of the old. These verses point beyond the temple to their fulfilment in Christ. But the principles remain the same. To come before God, there must be sacrifice and a faithful, pure priest.

Read Hebrews 9:11-14

Jesus is our faithful high priest. And the sacrifice that he offers is himself. His blood cleanses us in a way the blood of animals never could. Animals had to be sacrificed repeatedly every day (see Ezekiel 46:13-15). But Jesus' one sacrifice atones for ever! And that means we can be forgiven, cleansed and accepted into God's presence. We can come before God. And so now, for us, coming before God is easy. But it cost Jesus his life.

🔼 Pray
Read Hebrews 10:19-22

Sadly, prayer can often be a struggle for us—weak and sinful as we are. But since Christ's sacrifice has made it so simple for us to come before God, surely we should take up the struggle.

Talk to God about your thoughts now.

A new inheritance

Most of us have never been homeless. We can only imagine what it must feel like. Nowhere to sleep, nowhere to keep your possessions, nowhere to cook.

But also, no place in society, no address to give employers or libraries or other organisations. No sense of belonging.

But that means that Ezekiel calls on the powerful to end their oppression and corruption. What might that mean for you?

A new inheritance
Read Ezekiel 47:13-14

❓ *Why are boundaries important?*

The closing chapters of Ezekiel describe the allocation and boundaries of the land. (You can read the full details in 47:13 – 48:35.) More boring stuff? To us maybe. But to an Israelite the land was everything. It was your livelihood, your means of providing for the family. It was your link with the past; it gave you your identity. The land was God's gift to his people. Having a bit of the land meant you were part of God's people and a recipient of his blessing. And so you were very interested in how land was allocated; what belonged to who; who had a right to what.

No more oppression
Read Ezekiel 45:7-12

In the new creation, *everyone* will have enough. There will be no place for dispossession. No room for exploitation or corruption. That's good news for the poor and dispossessed of our world today. God's kingdom is a kingdom of justice and peace. The hungry are filled with good things, but the rich are sent away empty (Luke 1:51-53).

A safe haven
Read Ezekiel 47:21-23

❓ *Who is welcome in this kingdom?*

God ensures that there is a place for the dispossessed. This is not just for insiders. It would have been easy for the allocation of the land to exclude those who did not have the right pedigree. But God makes a point of including the refugees.

☑ Apply
Read 1 Peter 1:3-5

❓ *What is the inheritance that has been allotted to Christians?*
❓ *How should our inheritance affect our behaviour?*

All are welcome in God's kingdom—the dispossessed, refugees, the marginalised. This is what Jesus modelled. What about your church? Is it full of "respectable" people or does it include the socially marginalised?

☑ Pray

Ask God to fill you with gratitude for the inheritance that is yours in Christ.

JAMES: God's gym

Are you the real deal as a Christian, or are you deceiving yourself? What could be more important than finding out? That is what this letter is about.

Read James 1:1

Of the three people called James in the New Testament, the one who wrote this is probably James the half-brother of Jesus. He had been a sceptic but had come to recognise Jesus as Lord and Christ. The twelve tribes to whom he addressed his letter either referred to Jewish Christians or, more likely, to all God's people, the true Israel, scattered among the nations.

The trials of life

Read James 1:2

- ❓ *Give some examples of "trials of many kinds" which we might face as believers.*
- ❓ *How are we to respond? How does it make you feel, being told to do that?*

The testing of faith

Read James 1:3-4

- ❓ *Why can we "consider it pure joy"?*
- ❓ *In what ways does the testing of our faith benefit us?*

To get physically stronger, you have to put your muscles or cardiovascular system under pressure—by lifting weights or going running. The same is true of faith. Without being tested faith will be weak and unhealthy.

✅ Apply

Think of hardships you are going through at the moment, or have gone through in recent months. How might God have been using these difficulties to test and strengthen your faith? Give thanks to God for that.

The perspective of wisdom

Read James 1:5-8

The perspective on hardships in verses 2-4 is very different to how we naturally think. Wisdom is the ability to see life and trials God's way.

- ❓ *What should we do if we lack this wisdom and perspective?*
- ❓ *How does v 5 encourage us in asking?*
- ❓ *What is the warning in v 6-8?*
- ❓ *What is a "double-minded" person?*

Being double-minded is the same as being half-hearted. It's the Matthew 6:24 person who is trying to serve two masters.

🔼 Pray

Pray for wisdom from God to see the hardships you face as being ultimately for your good, and that God will use them to make you mature and complete as a Christian.

Pray that you will not be a half-hearted and double-minded Christian, but instead fully committed to the Lord.

The long view

Apparently, Elon Musk had read the entire Encyclopedia Britannica by the age of nine. But having knowledge is not the same as having wisdom. Wisdom enables us to see life from God's perspective.

In trials, look forward to the crown of life

Read James 1:9-12

- ❓ *What is meant by "believers in humble circumstances" (v 9)?*
- ❓ *What lies ahead for them if they persevere in faith under trial (v 12)?*
- ❓ *By contrast, what does the future hold for rich unbelievers (v 10-11)? In what ways are they like wild flowers?*

In the early church many believers were poor. They would have been tempted to envy rich unbelievers and give up on their faith. But wisdom sees the long-term perspective and the great reversal that will happen on the last day.

···· TIME OUT ··

"Stood the test" (v 12) translates a lovely little Greek word *dokimos*. It means to be tested and approved and shown to be genuine. If we persevere in faith, we will receive that stamp of approval.

▲ Pray

Pray for the wisdom to have this long-term perspective. Pray that you wouldn't envy unbelievers who seem to have it all now, but would persevere in faith. And if you are a rich Christian, pray that you would not trust in money, or try to serve two masters, but be generous.

In trials, hold on to the goodness of God

Read James 1:13-18

- ❓ *When we are going through hard times, in what ways might we be tempted to sin (from your own experience)?*
- ❓ *Where does such temptation not come from (v 13)?*
- ❓ *Where does it come from (v 14-15)?*

In hard times, we will be tempted to sin —to become angry and bitter, to take out our frustration on others, to seek escape in drink or pornography or a wrong relationship or buying things we don't need. But that isn't God's fault. Although God tests us, he doesn't tempt us.

- ❓ *What is the difference between testing and tempting?*

In times of trial, our view of God can get distorted. But we mustn't be deceived. He isn't some evil ogre tempting us to sin.

- ❓ *How do verses 16-18 emphasise the goodness of God?*

▲ Pray

Give thanks for the goodness of God as our loving heavenly Father. Pray that you won't lose sight of this when life is hard.

Mirror, mirror

In the art world some paintings are masterpieces worth a fortune, and others are worthless fakes. In the same way there are Christians who have genuine faith, and others who are deceiving themselves.

Receive the word
Read James 1:19-21

Verse 18 said that God "chose to give us birth through the word of truth". Now that word is likened to seed planted in us.

- ❷ *What should be our ongoing response to this implanted, saving word of the gospel (v 21b)?*
- ❷ *What does it look like to live it out (v 19-21a)?*

🔺 Pray

Reflect on these examples, and confess to God any ways in which you feel convicted of failing to live out the word. Give thanks for God's forgiveness in Christ, and pray for grace to live the righteous life God desires.

Be doers not just hearers
Read James 1:22-25

These verses contrast the person who only hears the word (v 22-24) with the person who does it (v 25).

- ❷ *In what sense are we "deceiving ourselves" (v 22) if we only hear the word? Deceiving ourselves about what?*
- ❷ *In what way is the hearer-only like someone who looks in a mirror?*
- ❷ *Instead how should we respond to the word (v 25)?*

⋯ TIME OUT ⋯
Read Matthew 7:24-27

- ❷ *What is the difference between the two builders in the parable Jesus told?*

☑ Apply

It's easy, when listening to sermons or sitting in Bible studies, to just hear—to treat the sermon like a performance to be given marks out of ten, or to find that by Monday morning you can't remember a thing about it.

- ❷ *What practical steps can we take to help ourselves, and one another, to be doers and not hearers only?*

Beware dead religion
Read James 1:26-27

- ❷ *What two types of religion are contrasted?*
- ❷ *What three examples does James give of true religion?*
- ❷ *What do they mean in practice?*

☑ Apply

In this passage we have looked in the mirror.

- ❷ *What have you seen?*
- ❷ *How are you going to respond?*

Kiss the King

Rebellion against God's king is madness. It will only lead to destruction. Instead everyone needs to serve, celebrate and embrace the king. But who is this king?

Read Psalm 2

Revolution

King David is on his throne—he is the anointed one of verse 2 (see Acts 4:25). David's kingdom was enormous, and included other nations who should have been delighted to be under the care of the one true God and his king, David.

> ❷ *What did the nations and their leaders think of David's rule?*
> ❸ *How do people reject God's rule today?*

The Father speaks

In a remarkable few verses, each person of the Trinity speaks. First the Father confirms the futility of rebellion: he "laughs", "scoffs", "rebukes" and "terrifies" (Psalm 2:3-5). It's sobering to think that rebellion is laughable and attracts the settled wrath of God. Why? Because of what God has already done—he has "installed" his king (v 6); and this king now speaks.

The Son speaks

The Lord's decree—his firm word—is now recounted by the son (v 7-9). It is a decree of absolute rule with no room for rebellion. For David, these words apply to his reign. However, the New Testament takes these verses and applies them again and again to King Jesus.

···**TIME OUT**····································

Check out some of the New Testament quotes of Psalm 2: **Acts 4:25-26, Acts 13:33 and Hebrews 1:5.**

The Spirit speaks

Acts 4:25 tells us that the Spirit inspired David to tell everybody how to respond to the Father's Son—the King. People must serve, celebrate and kiss the Son (i.e. acknowledge the King's right to rule them). This was a message about Israel's king; and, supremely, about *the* King, Jesus.

⌄ Apply

> ❷ *What makes it hard for you to celebrate the King's rule? How does this psalm help?*
> ❸ *What will it mean to let King Jesus rule over everything in your life?*

The rule of David is seen supremely in the reign of Jesus—and that's a reign every believer will share. The words of Psalm 2:9 are applied in Revelation 2:26-27 to the church.

⌃ Pray

Confess areas where you reject the King's rule and ask the Spirit to help you serve, celebrate and kiss the Son. Rejoice that one day this is a rule that you will share with him into all eternity.

No discrimination

Discrimination takes many forms, and it may be that we are more guilty of it ourselves than we think. It was a poison infecting the churches to whom James wrote this letter, and is still seen in churches today.

Evil thinking

Read James 2:1-4

> ❷ *What is the contrast between the two men in the example James gives? How are they treated differently?*
> ❷ *What does James say is wrong with such behaviour?*

The word translated "favouritism" is literally "face-taking". It's about making superficial judgments, and treating someone differently because of their appearance and our prejudices about that—their skin colour, race, ethnicity, sex, class, age, disabilities, or, as in this case, wealth.

⌄ Apply

Two people walk into your church just before the service—one is a homeless man, smelling of sweat and cigarettes, and the other is a beautiful young professional woman who has just parked a smart car outside.

> ❷ *Do you think you would treat them differently? Why?*

···· TIME OUT ····

Read 1 Samuel 16:1-13

> ❷ *In what ways do both Jesse and Samuel show favouritism based on appearance? How is God different?*

As soon as we meet someone new, we instinctively assess how to respond to them based on superficial factors—their appearance, age, social status, nationality. As believers in the Lord Jesus we need to beware being "judges with evil thoughts" who discriminate in how we treat people—at church, at home and at work.

Strange behaviour

Read James 2:5-7

> ❷ *Why was it very strange for believers to discriminate against the poor (v 5-6a)?*
> ❷ *And why was it equally odd to show favouritism to the rich (v 6b-7)?*

Our world assigns value to people based on their wealth, success, status, education. But the values of God's kingdom are different. He delights to choose poor people, whom the world overlooks, to be rich in faith.

⌃ Pray

Confess times when you have been guilty of discrimination in how you have treated people, and been no different to the world and its value system.

Pray that God would enable you by his Spirit to see people as he sees them—and to treat them accordingly.

Blessed are the merciful

We may think that showing favouritism is not a big deal, and not something to worry about. But that is not how God sees things.

Breaking the law
Read James 2:8-11

- ❓ *In what way is showing favouritism breaking God's law?*
- ❓ *What do verses 10-11 say to the person who might respond, "Ok, I do show favouritism. But there are much worse sins. And in lots of others ways I do keep God's law."?*

If you lay a pane of glass on the ground and jump up and down on it, smashing it into tiny pieces, it's useless. But if you're carrying a pane of glass and trip up and drop it so that it cracks in two, that's also broken and useless. God's law is like that sheet of glass. Even if we break it in just one point, we are still convicted as law-breakers and are guilty of sin.

⌄ Apply

Instead of trying to play down or excuse our showing of favouritism, we need to confess it to God, ask his forgiveness and turn from it. The final verses of this passage leave us in no doubt about how important it is that we do so.

Judged by the law
Read James 2:12-13

- ❓ *What does it mean that we will be "judged by the law" on the last day?*
- ❓ *How should that affect our behaviour?*
- ❓ *What will happen to those who through favouritism and discrimination have not been merciful to others?*
- ❓ *How does this echo the teaching of Jesus in Matthew 5:7?*

As sinners we are saved by faith, not by our works. But genuine faith will be seen in how we live. And one of the fruits of true faith is that we are merciful to others. A faith lacking this will be exposed in the end as fake. Such people will receive judgment without mercy. If I want God to be merciful to me, I need to be merciful to others. Such mercy will triumph over God's judgment.

⌃ Pray

Merciful Lord, looking in the mirror of your word has exposed the ugliness of how sometimes I treat people with favouritism.

I don't want just to walk away and forget.

Please forgive me through your Son, and empower me by your Spirit to be merciful and loving to all I meet.

Amen

Useless faith

Once, when about to board a long-haul flight, I was turned away at the gate because of a passport hitch. It was a sickening experience. But imagine being turned away at the gates of heaven.

One reason James wrote this letter was to prevent that happening to any of us. In the rest of chapter 2 he distinguishes two types of faith—faith that doesn't save and faith that does. The verses today look at the first type.

Damned faith

Read James 2:14-20

- ❓ *What is the answer to the two questions (v 14)?*
- ❓ *What examples has James already given in the letter of deeds which are the fruit of true faith (1:19-21; 26-28; 2:1, 8)?*

Disengaged faith

- ❓ *What is wrong with this person's reaction to the Christian brother or sister in need?*

Words *do* matter and are very powerful (see 1:26), but words to other people, or words to God about other people are no substitute for practical action. Love gets involved.

···· TIME OUT ·································

Read Matthew 25:31-46

- ❓ *What is the contrast...*
  - *in how they treated other believers?*
  - *in how they themselves are treated by God in eternity?*

Dead and divorced faith

- ❓ *What is the sign of a dead body / faith (James 2:17, 26)?*
- ❓ *What is wrong with the views in v 14?*

The "someone" in verse 14 claims to have faith without deeds. A different "someone" (v 18a) claims to have deeds without faith. Both agree that faith and deeds can be separated. In verse 18b James responds to the verse 14 person. He affirms that faith and deeds can never be divorced from each other.

Demonic faith

- ❓ *In what way is faith without deeds no different to the kind of faith that demons have (v 19)?*
- ❓ *What is James' conclusion (v 20)?*

In this passage James throws some hard punches. But he does so in love, to save us from having the shock of our lives at the gates of heaven.

☑ Apply

Does the evidence in your life indicate a dead or living faith? Ask someone who knows you well what they think. If living, give thanks to God for his mercy to you. If dead, come to Christ, and ask God to give you the gift of faith and his Spirit.

Faith in action

*It is not enough just to say that we have faith in Christ. Genuine faith must also be
lived out and make a difference to our daily lives.*

Apparent contradiction
Read James 2:21-26

- ❷ *According to these verses, on what basis
  is a person considered righteous by God
  (v 21, 24, 25)?*
- ❷ *How does that appear to contradict
  Ephesians 2:8-9 (or Romans 3:28;
  Galatians 2:16)?*
- ❷ *How would you explain how the two
  truths go together?*

James and Paul were addressing different
problems. Paul was often up against people
who thought they could get right with God
through what they did, so he emphasised
that salvation is through faith alone. James
was addressing people who claimed to have
faith in Jesus but whose lives were unchanged, so he emphasised good deeds as
the evidence of a living faith.

Paul's focus was more on how you become
a Christian, and James' focus was on how
you know you are a true Christian. Both
agree that we are declared in the right with
God through faith in Jesus, but if that faith
is genuine it will be demonstrated in what
we do.

Inspiring examples

James gives two examples of such genuine,
faith—a Jewish man and a Gentile woman.

- ❷ *God made promises to Abraham
  (Genesis 15:5-6). How did Abraham
  respond (James 2:23)? What was the
  result (v 23)?*
- ❷ *Many years later (Genesis 22) how did
  Abraham demonstrate his faith (James
  2:21)? What was the significance of this
  (v 22)?*
- ❷ *How did the prostitute Rahab also
  demonstrate that she had a living faith
  (v 25; Joshua 2)?*
- ❷ *What point do they both illustrate
  (James 2:26)?*

Lived out faith could have cost Abraham the
life of his son, and Rahab her own life.

☑ Apply

Two accusations levelled by unbelievers are
(a) that Christians are hypocrites, because
Christians they know seem to be no different to others, and (b) that Christianity is too
easy, because with a free ticket to heaven
you can do what you want. How could you
respond, using what we've learned in this
study (and the previous one) about dead
faith and living faith?

☑ Pray

Pray that like Abraham and Rahab your actions would demonstrate a living faith; that
by the Spirit your faith would bear much
fruit today.

Restless evil

We often downplay the importance of what we say. "I didn't mean it." "I was only joking." "Actions speak louder than words". But our words matter. They reveal whether or not our faith is genuine.

James has already mentioned that an uncontrolled tongue is one symptom of worthless religion (1:26). He now takes a deep dive into our mouths.

Dangerous influence
Read James 3:1-6

❓ *Why is Bible teaching a dangerous profession (v 1)?*

Words are very powerful, and so if your tongue is your main tool in your job, you can do a huge amount of good or bad.

⌃ Pray

Do pray for the Bible teachers in your church, that they would take great care in what they say and teach.

❓ *What encouragement is there for us in verse 2 when we fail in what we say?*

The tongue may be small—just 0.045% of your body-weight—but it has an influence way out of proportion to its size.

❓ *How do the three illustrations highlight this? Which is the odd one out?*
- *Horses (v 3)*
- *Ships (v 4)*
- *Fires (v 5-6)*

❓ *Give some examples how words, like a spark starting a forest fire, can cause widespread devastation.*

⌄ Apply

Confess to God ways in which your words have caused damage—gossip, slander, lies, boasting, making fun of someone, putting someone down, destroying someone's reputation or self-confidence. Ask God for forgiveness through the Son, and for power to control your tongue through the Spirit.

TIME OUT

The book of Proverbs has much to say about the power of our words. Look up these verses:
- The power of the tongue: Proverbs 18:21
- Misuse of the tongue: 12:25; 15:1; 24:26
- Good use of words: 11:9; 18:7-8; 29:5
- Tips for the tongue: 10:19; 13:3; 15:28; 18:2, 13; 29:20.

Humanly untameable

Resolving to take care in what we say is good but not enough.

Read James 3:7-8

❓ *What can we tame (v 7)? Give some examples.*
❓ *What can't we tame (v 8)? In what way is the tongue like a spitting cobra?*

⌄ Pray

Lord, please, by your Spirit, tame my tongue so it will only speak words of truth and love.

The source

Sometimes, when you go for a check-up, the doctor will tell you to stick out your tongue—because often sickness inside us can be detected on the tongue. The same is true for us spiritually.

Unnaturally inconsistent

Read James 3:9-12

- ❷ *What inconsistency does James highlight in how we use our tongues (v 9-10)?*
- ❷ *What two illustrations does he use to show how unnatural this is (v 11-12)?*
- ❷ *Where do the illustrations suggest the problem is do you think?*

✔ Apply

Do you see such inconsistency with your own tongue? Are you using it one minute to praise and pray to God, and then the next minute to swear at another driver, to spread gossip, or to lie to cover up something you've done? Is this a pattern rather than an occasional slip?

Disturbingly revealing

Read James 3:13-18

- ❷ *What two wrong attitudes does James identify in the heart (v 14, 16)?*
- ❷ *What does it lead to (v 15-16)?*
- ❷ *How does "the wisdom that comes from heaven" contrast with such "earthly" behaviour (v 17-18)?*

---- TIME OUT ----

What does Jesus teach about this in **Matthew 7:17-18** and **12:33-37**?

Our words reveal what our hearts are like—whether we are people of earthly or heavenly wisdom. If my tongue is doing a lot of damage, the root of the problem is not my tongue but my heart, my inner person. If our hearts are renewed by the Spirit, that will overflow in words that are good—that speak truth, and build up, and are loving—albeit none of us is perfect, and we will still sometimes say things we shouldn't (James 3:2).

✔ Apply

Jesus said of the final judgment, "By your words you will be acquitted, and by your words you will be condemned" (Matthew 12:37).

- ❷ *Do you think your words will acquit or condemn you?*

⌃ Pray

If you think you would be acquitted by your words, give thanks that God by his Spirit has renewed your heart with heavenly wisdom. And pray that you would continue to use your tongue for good.

If condemned, pray that God would have mercy on you now through Jesus, and pour his heavenly wisdom into your heart by his Spirit. Jesus said, "Make a tree good and its fruit will be good". Ask God to change you into a good tree! And then pray Psalm 141:3.

Sleep well

Those who trust King Jesus have confidence of final deliverance and eternal blessing.

Read Psalm 3

This short psalm is made up of three little sections, all of which conclude with the Hebrew word *selah* (end v 2, 4, 8). Each tells us something of the mind of King David as he fled Jerusalem from his son Absalom, who had rebelled against his father.

Many foes

Verses 1 and 2 of the psalm give us a vivid picture of just what David is up against. It's not just Absalom. Each of the three sentences begin with the same idea: "many". David is really up against it. Nor are these just silent foes. They are rising up against him and spreading rumours that he is not God's anointed king (v 2).

❷ *How would most people respond to such danger?*

···· TIME OUT ··

To understand what David is facing...

Read 2 Samuel 15 – 16

Confident assurance

❷ *How does David respond (Psalm 3:3-4)?*

We might expect panic or desperation—after all, this is a king on the run for his life. But no—David still believes the promises of God and that God surrounds him with glorious protection. David's enemies may

cause him to bow his head in shame, but his glorious God lifts his head up.

Assured deliverance

Having expressed this assurance, David can now get a good night's sleep. Verses 5 and 6 are remarkable, as anybody who is facing uncertainty can testify. It is David's knowledge of the character of God that allows him to rest, despite the desperate situation he finds himself in. His prayer (v 7) is a covenant prayer asking God to do what he has promised and make his enemies literally toothless. As this prayer is answered, David knows that he will again experience the covenant blessings of the Lord.

This prayer was also prayed by another King in David's line. His enemies were also many. Many scoffed as he hung upon the cross. But he entrusted himself to his Father's care, confidently knowing that he would be delivered from death. Christians can share David's confidence because King Jesus has prayed this prayer.

◪ Pray

Re-read the whole psalm and use it to pray. Whatever dangers you face, you can be confident in God's final deliverance and blessing. Your enemies have been put under Jesus' feet and so you can sleep, confident in his sovereign rule over your life.

War and peace

Conflict is all around us in the world—between nations, within communities, in workplaces, inside the home, in marriages. But conflict among believers should cause us great concern.

....

Conflict with others

Read James 4:1-3

Sometimes people look back with longing at the days of the early church, thinking how amazing it must have been to be part of it. But all was not well.

❷ *What was causing fights and quarrels among the believers (v 1-2a)?*

❷ *What examples has James already given of such sinful desires in our hearts (see 3:14,16; see also 1 Peter 2:11)?*

The cause of conflict goes much deeper than us being tired or under pressure. It is the sinful desires in our hearts—selfish ambition, jealousy, envy, coveting—which overflow in conflict with others. Conflict with others comes from conflict in us.

···· **TIME OUT** ···

Read Galatians 2:11-14

Not all conflict between believers is an overflow of sinful desires in our hearts. Sometimes conflict is necessary and right in confronting wrong belief or behaviour.

⌄ Apply

It's not wrong to disagree with someone, but so easily disagreement can escalate into sinful conflict in the way we go about it. Think back to the last quarrel or fight you had. What was it about? What sinful desires

in your heart were at work?

❷ *How could praying have made a difference (James 4:2b-3)?*

Conflict with God

Read James 4:4-5

❷ *In what sense is engaging in sinful conflict "friendship with the world"?*

❷ *How does being worldly like this affect our relationship with God?*

❷ *Why does behaving like this make us "adulterous people"? Why is God rightly 'jealous'?*

If as believers we fight and quarrel, driven by sinful desires in our hearts, we are behaving just like the unbelieving world around us. Such worldliness makes us enemies of God. In God's sight such behaviour is firstly murder (v 2), because we are being hostile to others (see Matthew 5:21-22); and secondly adultery, because we are being spiritually unfaithful to him. These verses should make us re-evaluate how serious it is to have conflict among believers.

⌃ Pray

Think back to a recent occasion when sinful desires in your heart overflowed into conflict with someone. Pray for God's forgiveness, and for power to be "peacemakers who sow in peace" (James 3:18).

Conflict resolution

Ungodly conflict with one another is a serious business, as such worldliness puts us in conflict with God himself. So we need to urgently sort out our relationships, starting with God.

Start with God
Read James 4:6-10

> ❷ *What is the first step in conflict resolution?*
> ❷ *What reasons are given for doing this (v 6, 10)?*

So much conflict with others is fuelled by pride. Our pride causes things to escalate because we won't back down, instead wanting to win the argument and prove ourselves to be right. Pride means we take offence easily and seek the limelight. Pride resents it when someone else patronises me. But God hates pride. He opposes the proud. As C.S. Lewis said, it is "the complete anti-God state of mind".

⌄ Apply

Think back to the last time you had an argument or other conflict with someone. How did pride make things worse?

Three pairs of commands in verses 7-9 unpack what it looks like to submit ourselves humbly to God.

> ❷ *What might it mean in practice for you to resist the devil and draw near to God (v 7b-8a)?*
> ❷ *In what sense are we to wash our hands and purify our hearts (v 8b)? (The clue is in the references to "you sinners" and "you double-minded".)*

> ❷ *Over what do you think we are to grieve and mourn (v 9)?*

⌃ Pray

Pride is something with which we all struggle. Confess to God now your pride, and humbly draw near to him. Turn from wrong behaviour and wrong desires. And ask for God's forgiveness and power to change.

Then with others
Read James 4:11-12

> ❷ *What do we need to stop doing (v 11a)? Why (v 11b; see also 2:8)?*

If our sinful desires are overflowing in conflict and speaking evil of other believers, then we're not loving them as God's law says we should. And when we do this, we are also sitting in judgment on them.

> ❷ *Why is that not a wise move (v 12)?*

⌃ Pray

Give thanks that a world without conflict is on its way, when Christ returns. Pray that as God's people we will live in harmony now as the community of the future—loving him and one another. Pray for God's grace to sort out your relationship with him and with others.

What is your life?

A mark of genuine faith is to not be worldly. Chapter 4 so far has exposed worldliness seen in conflict. James now focuses on worldliness in how we make plans.

Godless plans

Read James 4:13-17

❓ *What plans does the business person make in verse 13? What is wrong with their planning?*

This isn't saying it's wrong to plan. In business you've got to make plans; you can't just live one day at a time. The issue here is the attitude—*leaving God out of the picture* (which we'll get to in v 15); *pride* (which we'll get to in v 16); and *living life without reference to God*; as if you are in control.

⌄ Apply

❓ *Why is it even more of a temptation for us in our 21ˢᵗ-century society to live as if we don't need God, and leave him out of the picture?*

Uncertain life

❓ *Verse 14 says that we do not know what will happen tomorrow. What might happen tomorrow?*

❓ *What is the point of comparing our lives to mist? What makes it such a powerful picture? How does it contrast with how we tend to think of our lives?*

Think of the steam coming out of a kettle; or your breath outside on a cold day; or the morning mist over the fields; or a puff of smoke coming out of a chimney. It's here for just a very brief moment and then is gone. This is you and me.

Divine will

❓ *Given that life is so uncertain, what should our attitude be (v 15)?*

❓ *What reality are we acknowledging when we have this attitude?*

⌄ Apply

Sometimes Christians say, "I'll see you next week, God willing", or they write "D.V.", which is the Latin for "God willing" (*deo volente*).

❓ *Do you think this is a helpful practice? Why / why not?*

Evil pride

❓ *What heart attitude is exposed when we live as if we are in charge (v 16-17)?*

⌃ Pray

Pray that your faith will be reflected in a godly, humble perspective on life—knowing that life is brief, God is in charge, and everything is subject to his will.

Silver and gold

It's been said that the last part of a person to be converted is their wallet or purse—but until it is, there is no living faith. Money, and what we do with it, is a spiritual issue.

Weep and wail
Read James 5:1-6

❓ *How is the coming judgement described in these verses?*

The Bible does not condemn people for being rich, but it does condemn those who misuse their wealth.

❓ *What are the rich condemned for in verses 3 and 5?*
❓ *What are they condemned for in verses 4 and 6?*

···· **TIME OUT** ·································

❓ *Why do you think the city of Sodom was destroyed? Now read Ezekiel 16:49.*
❓ *Is that different to what you answered?*

Read Luke 16:19-31

❓ *How does the fate of the rich man in this parable illustrate how serious the issue is that James is addressing?*

⌄ Apply

The rich in James chapter 5 are unbelievers, living lives of self-indulgence and luxury, whilst ignoring or oppressing the poor. But if we are rich believers, we too need to take the warning here to heart. What would you say is the biggest threat to your faith? We hear plenty about sexual immorality, but perhaps less about the love of money. Biblically though, it is just as dangerous.

Be patient and persevere
Read James 5:7-11

Many of these early believers were poor, and were being exploited by wealthy unbelievers.

❓ *Pick out the three references to being patient. For what are we to wait patiently?*
❓ *In what way are we to be like the farmer (v 7-8)?*
❓ *What mustn't we do (v 9)?*
❓ *How should the Old Testament prophets and Job inspire us (v 10-11)?*

Lord Shaftesbury, the great English social reformer of the 19th century, was born into privilege as an aristocrat. But on coming to Christ, instead of living a life of luxury and self-indulgence, he served the poor, oppressed and exploited, and the cause of overseas missions. He said, "I do not think that in the last forty years I have ever lived one conscious hour that was not influenced by the thought of our Lord's return".

⌃ Pray

Pray that the prospect of the Lord's return would consciously shape your use of money and your treatment of the poor. Pray for patience and endurance in obedient faith, especially in difficult times.

Prayer and praise

Pressure can be a making or breaking experience. Which one it turns out to be, depends on how we respond. But good times bring their own pitfalls as well. This passage tells us how to respond.

Prayer

Read James 5:12-13

❷ *What do you think verse 12 means by "do not swear"? Why is that a temptation when we're under pressure?*

James' letter has had a lot to say about controlling our tongues, so using bad language and taking God's name in vain (saying OMG, for example) are inappropriate for true believers. But the particular focus here is on swearing in taking oaths—saying to God "If you get me out of this mess, I promise I'll..." We're not to bargain with God like that. It can land us in big trouble, as Jephthah found (Judges 11), because an oath is a serious business.

❷ *What are we to do instead, when we're going through hard times (James 5:13a)?*

···· **TIME OUT** ··

Look up these others verses on prayer in times of trouble: **Philippians 4:6-7; 1 Peter 5:7; Psalm 50:15.**

🔽 Apply

What pressures are you facing at the moment? There are lots of wrong ways we will be tempted to respond: to just grin and bear it; to complain and grumble; to bottle it up and retreat into ourselves; to lie awake turning it over in our minds; to use foul language and lash out at others; to take oaths to bargain with God; to turn to drink or pornography. Instead we should pray—in James 5:13-18 prayer is mentioned in every verse. Pray to the Lord now about your situation.

Praise

❷ *What are we to do when life is good and we are happy? What would this look like in everyday life (v 13b)?*
❷ *Read Deuteronomy 8:11-18. What did Moses warn the people about on the edge of the promised land?*

If there's a danger of neglecting prayer when life is hard, there's an equally big danger of neglecting praise when life is good—turning to him when we're in need, but ignoring him when we're happy.

🔼 Pray

Pray that prayer and praise will become the rhythm of your everyday life—as natural as breathing in and out—bringing your needs to God in prayer, and bringing your thanks to him in praise.

In it together

Keeping going and growing as Christians is not a lone pursuit—it's a community project. We need one another.

Is anyone ill?

Read James 5:14-18

> ❷ *What are we to do when we fall ill (v 14)?*
> ❷ *What will the Lord do (v 15)?*
> ❷ *Why do you think confession of sin is encouraged in this situation (v 16)?*

The point of calling the church elders is not that they have special powers, but that they represent the church family. By calling them to pray, you're asking the church to pray for you.

Anointing with oil was a common practice in first-century culture in a way that it isn't in ours today. The only other place in the New Testament that anointing with oil is mentioned in connection with healing is Mark 6:13. So whether we are to do such anointing today is debatable.

···· **TIME OUT** ··

Not everyone is healed who prays in faith for healing or who is prayed for. And not being healed is not necessarily because of lack of faith. The apostle Paul was a godly man of strong faith—yet **read 2 Corinthians 12:7-9**. We pray in faith but acknowledge that God is sovereign.

> ❷ *How does the example of Elijah encourage us in our praying (James 5:16-18)?*

> ❷ *How do these verses counter the objection "But Elijah was a great prophet, and I'm not"?*

▾ Apply

Pray now for any fellow believers you know who are ill, that the Lord would heal them. And when you are ill, instead of suffering alone in silence, reach out to your church family and leaders, and ask them to pray *for* you and *with* you.

Is anyone wandering?

Read James 5:19-20

> ❷ *In what ways do you think someone might "wander from the truth"? What examples have we had in this letter?*
> ❷ *What responsibility does each of us have towards such a wanderer?*
> ❷ *Why is it important that we take action?*

James' big concern in this letter has been to bring back wandering believers to a true, living, obedient faith. This is something all of us are to do, not just church leaders.

▴ Pray

Pray that you yourself would remain on the true path in belief and behaviour. Pray for any wanderers you know, that the Lord might use you to bring them back.

Peace in trouble

Though David—the anointed king—feels surrounded, he still experiences deep and lasting peace. And so can we.

Read Psalm 4

❓ *What evidence do you see (e.g. repeated words) that this psalm is closely linked to Psalm 3?*

Enemies (again)

Psalm 4 echoes much of the previous psalm and is probably from the same time in David's life. He is still beset by enemies and cries out to his "righteous God" for help (v 1). The phrase "give me relief" literally means "enlarge my narrow places"—in other words, David feels cornered.

❓ *What situations in life make you feel trapped like David?*

Who's cornered?

These enemies have robbed the king of his glory (v 2) and are pursuing lies (an alternative way to translate "false gods"). But the last laugh is with David. To all intents and purposes he may appear to be the one who is trapped, but in fact it is his enemies who are truly cornered. Verse 3 explains why. David is the anointed king whom God has set apart, and God will surely hear his prayer.

This is a complete turnaround, as David makes clear in verses 4-5. Rather than David shaking with fear, it is his enemies who should be trembling. David preaches to them: *Don't sin! Search your hearts! Be silent! Trust God!*

The promise still holds

Of course, it does not seem that way to outsiders. No wonder they are asking questions (v 6). But the original promise of Numbers 6:25, which is repeated in the second half of Psalm 4:6, is still true. And therefore David can pray for joy and express a deep and lasting peace. Despite all evidence to the contrary, he is not cornered.

⌄ Apply

This is another song sung by our King, Jesus. His own people, the Jews, sought delusions and lies and turned his glory to shame—or so they thought. And yet the Father did shine his face upon him. Jesus rose from the grave to bring peace and security to every believer.

❓ *Look back at the situations you listed earlier. How do the death and resurrection of Jesus change how you think about these?*

⌃ Pray

Thank God that he set apart his faithful servant, Jesus. And thank God that he hears his Son's prayers for his people. Pray for the joy and peace that result.

ZEPHANIAH: Extremes

Zephaniah comes last alphabetically and perhaps last in familiarity. It's a book of extremes, speaking explicitly of the horror of judgment alongside the wonder of salvation.

Read Zephaniah 1:1-6

A notable genealogy

Read Zephaniah 1:1 again

We know more about Zephaniah than any other Old Testament prophet, his genealogy stretches back four generations.

> ❷ *Which names do you recognise in the genealogy?*

Zephaniah's great-great-grandfather was Judah's good king Hezekiah who reigned 60 years before Zephaniah's day. This introduction also places Zephaniah as speaking during the time of Josiah, Judah's good, young, reforming king. Between Hezekiah and Josiah, Judah has gone through a dark time under Manasseh and Amon.

···· **TIME OUT** ····································

Read 2 Kings 21 to find out what has happened between Hezekiah and Josiah.

> ❷ *Judgment is coming anyway, so why does God send Zephaniah to speak now?*

A terrifying start

Read Zephaniah 1:2-6 again

> ❷ *Which words are repeated in these 5 verses?*

What is pictured in verses 2-3 is judgment similar to the flood in Noah's day. In fact it is even worse than that. In the middle of

verse 3 we learn that even the fish will not escape this time. This is ultimate judgment— de-creation—pictured on a global scale as God reverses days 5 and 6 of Genesis 1.

> ❷ *What reasons are given for this judgment in Zephaniah 1:4-6?*
> ❷ *How many times does Zephaniah note this is God speaking?*

Verse 4 points out that some in Judah and Jerusalem are idolatrous, a remnant of Baal worshippers with their own priests. Verse 5 highlights two failings of God's people: some are bowing down to the sun, moon and stars, while others are syncretists, swearing by the LORD but *also* swearing by Malkam, the Canaanite God worshipped through child sacrifice.

There are also those (verse 6), who have given up following God all together: those who have ceased seeking the Lord and ceased enquiring of the Lord. It is a sorry picture of God's chosen people, so complacent, compromised and confused in their worship of their covenant God.

> ❷ *How would you feel if you were God looking down on your chosen people and seeing them behave in this way?*

🔺 Pray

Give thanks for God's patience and his grace in warning people before judgment comes.

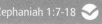

Judgment described

Alarms sound to get people to act while there is still time. Zephaniah is an alarm going off to get the people of Judah to respond before judgment falls.

Read Zephaniah 1:7-18

❷ *How many times is the word "day" used in these verses?*

Verse 7 is alarming! The day of the Lord described will see Judah treated by God as a sacrifice with the consecrated guest (the Babylonians) sweeping in to sack the city. It will be a terrifying day of punishment. Verse 10 also shows the extent of the judgment. The Fish Gate is on the outer periphery of the city whereas the New Quarter (v 10) is the city centre. The hills are mentioned, which are the high places surrounding the city and the Mortar is mentioned which is the area of quarrying (or perhaps the market—see NIV footnote). The message is that this judgment will permeate the whole city.

❷ *What sort of people will be caught up in this judgment according to verse 12?*

TIME OUT

Read Deuteronomy 28:20

❷ *How does this verse explain the cause of this judgment that is soon to arrive?*

Zephaniah 1:14-18 is a poem describing the day of the Lord. It is a terrifying picture. However, not everything described here was enacted through the Babylonian invasion: there are in fact at least two "days" described. The immediate day when the Babylonians will conquer Judah, but a greater

more final day when God judges the world. We are living between these two days.

❷ *What does this passage teach you about God's attitude to sin and justice?*
❷ *How does what is pictured here make you feel?*

Zephaniah was warning his nation that the judgment promised as a result of Manasseh's reign (2 Kings 21), will soon arrive. Jerusalem will soon face judgment. However, the greater day pictured is still to come, a day we need to be alert to, ready for and quickened by. A day when God will judge the earth, right all wrongs, punish all iniquity and win final victory over all his enemies. It is therefore crucial that we do not go about our lives complacently assuming that this day is never coming. Zephaniah is still speaking to us to warn us.

Apply
Read Acts 17:29-31

❷ *How should you respond in view of the coming judgment?*

Judgment avoided?

The prophet has alerted us to the judgment that is coming. He now tells us what to do in the face of such judgment. It is time for immediate and drastic action.

Gather

Read Zephaniah 2:1-3

❓ *Which words are repeated in this passage?*

❓ *Which two commands are given to the people of Judah in these three verses?*

❓ *How are God's people described?*

❓ *How is the day of the LORD described?*

This passage at the beginning of chapter 2 sees the very first glimmer of hope in the whole book. Chapter 1 has been a detailed description of God's righteous anger poured out on his complacent, confused and compromised people. Here however, there is the potential for reprieve. Even now at the eleventh hour, with the day of the LORD fast approaching, there is the possibility of being hidden, being sheltered, being safe when "the day" comes. God's grace is extended to a "shameful nation".

There are two commands, *Gather* and *Seek*. Gathering involves all the people assembling together, as well as gathering themselves, preparing themselves for major exertion as drastic change is needed. Seek is equivalent to repentance: turning from their wicked ways and returning to their covenant God. Chapter 1 catalogues an array of failings of God's people and their only hope is to seek the Lord, proclaims Zephaniah.

It is amazing to see the mercy of God in Zephaniah. God's people have been idolatrous, syncretistic (they have mixed other religious thinking and practices with the worship of God), apostate and complacent. And yet even now God wants to show mercy to them if only they would respond to Zephaniah's message.

Zephaniah's message will only be responded to by humble people (2:3). This is a major theme in Zephaniah, God will cut down the proud and lift up the humble. These humble people are the obedient ones who have obeyed him and followed his commands. Here again are the first signs of a faithful remnant amidst a faithless people.

···TIME OUT···

Read Luke 13:34-35

❓ *How is Jesus looking over Jerusalem similar to Zephaniah's message here at the beginning of chapter 2?*

⌃ Pray

Give thanks for God's mercy and grace towards us in the Lord Jesus.

Pray that we would be those who grow in humility and obedience.

Pray that we would be those who would long to see others gathered under the shelter of the cross, in view of the coming judgment.

The nations nullified

Judgment began with God's people but now it ripples out to the surrounding nations. By the end of this chapter none of God's people will be in any doubt as to who God is.

Read Zephaniah 2:4-15

Philistia

The first nation judged is Philistia (v 4-7), to the east of Judah, represented by her four major cities. This warrior civilisation and historic enemy of God's people will be flattened.

Moab and Ammon

Second are Moab and Ammon (v 8-11), to the west of Judah, a people related to Judah. Moab and Ammon were the sons born to Lot and his daughters after their incest (Genesis 19). These peoples that escaped from Sodom and Gomorrah will become as Sodom and Gomorrah.

> ❓ *What is the reason given for their judgment (v 8, 10)?*

The word "destroys in verse 11 is literally the word shrivel. God defeating his enemies is as simple as throwing a crisp packet on a fire.

Cush

Cush (v 12) is as far south from Judah as one could imagine in these days. This faraway nation will not escape judgment either.

Assyria

Even the superpower Assyria, to the north

of Judah, will be destroyed and become a desolation (v 13-15).

> ❓ *What reason is given for this (v 15)?*

Zephaniah speaks of this judgment rippling out to all nations, symbolised by the four countries mentioned (east, west, north south). God asserts his sovereignty over the whole earth.

However there is hope for God's people mixed in with this global judgment.

Hope

Read Zephaniah 2:7, 9 again

> ❓ *What will the judgement of the nations mean for God's remnant people?*

⌄ Apply

Zephaniah 2:4-15 has a mix of God's justice and love, his judgment and salvation, the destruction of his enemies and restoration of his people.

> ❓ *Why do we need to understand both?*
> ❓ *Are you in danger of focusing too much on one of these characteristics?*

There is also the hint that some from the nations will be saved (v 11). Even as God's people are being judged, there will be many Gentiles who will worship God rightly. Zephaniah glimpses vaguely what John would see clearly in the book of Revelation.

The city summoned

Zephaniah's message of judgment to God's people in Judah now reaches its climax. We see Jerusalem summoned to the dock and charged by God for her shameless rebellion.

Summoned

Read Zephaniah 3:1-5

At first reading, chapter 3 seems to be speaking about Nineveh—the city referred to at the end of chapter 2. However, on closer inspection, verses 2 and 5 show that the camera angle has changed and it is Jerusalem that is now being described.

What a terrible state Jerusalem is in! Insolent, listening to no voice. Obstinate, accepting no correction. With predatory officials, fickle prophets and profane priests all adding to the rebellion, the defilement and the oppression.

❓ *How is God contrasted with the city (v 5)?*

Reminded

Read Zephaniah 3:6-7

In verse 6 God reminds his people of his care; how he had won victories against their enemies. They only need to think back some 60 years to God's rescue of Jerusalem from Sennacherib and the Assyrians.

❓ *How did God expect the people of Judah to respond to these victories (v 7)?*
❓ *How did they actually respond?*

Sentenced

Read Zephaniah 3:8

God's patience has been exhausted by his shameless, unrepentant people. Therefore he commands them to wait. Waiting is usually associated with perseverance, dependence and continuing to hope in God. Here however it is used in terms of waiting for judgment, like the naughty school child waiting outside the headteacher's study. The image is of indignation, burning anger and ferocious jealousy.

⌄ Apply

❓ *How does this passage make you feel?*
❓ *How often do you think about God's righteous anger towards sin and the judgment that he promises?*

Against the black backdrop of judgment the gospel shines all the brighter. In the Lord Jesus we have one who is our substitute, one who had poured out on him the burning anger and indignation of his Father on account of our sin. He was judged so we could be acquitted, he was seized so that we might go free.

⌃ Pray

Give thanks that God is righteous and perfectly just and in the end he guarantees that justice will be done.

Give thanks for Jesus who enables God to be just and justifier of repentant people.

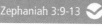
God's people gathered

There is now a remarkable key change in Zephaniah. We move from E flat minor to G major. What has been severe judgment for two and a half chapters now crescendos into an awesome vista of blessing.

Unity

Read Zephaniah 3:9-10

God now steps in and a remarkable transformation happens. The first thing God does is to transform the speech of the peoples to a pure speech, uniting a diverse and dispersed people. Now with one language they can all call on the name of the Lord and serve him with one accord.

TIME OUT

Read Genesis 11:1-9

❷ *How is Zephaniah 3:9-10 a reversal of the Babel curse?*

These peoples are gathered from far and wide. Those mentioned here are from beyond the rivers of Cush. This would be the ends of the earth for Judah. From even here God will gather worshippers to be among his people. The word "scattered" is exactly the same word used in Genesis 11.

⌄ Apply

If God by his transforming grace is able to gather the peoples of the earth together to worship him as one, what excuses do we have when there is disunity in our local churches?

Humility

Read Zephaniah 3:11-12

These people are not gathered because they are sinless but because they are repentant. Their rebellious deeds will not result in shame. Again we see God blessing the humble and opposing the proud. The proudly exultant ones will be removed and the humble and lowly will be left—those who have sought refuge in the name of the Lord.

❷ *Is humility and lowliness valued in our world?*

Safety

Read Zephaniah 3:13

These remnant people are now transformed and act as God himself acts in verse 5. They do no injustice and speak no lies. And not only that, this people will find rest and safety for ever at the end of verse 13. It's a thrilling picture of a transformed life, with God, in a new creation. A day is coming when God will judge the world, gather his people, forgive their sins, transform them and give them rest for ever.

We now know that God accomplished this plan through the sending of his Son Jesus for us.

❷ *How does this picture painted by Zephaniah make you feel?*

God's people restored

A book that has contained some of the starkest images of judgment in the Bible now gives way to some of the most beautiful imagery in the whole Old Testament.

Zephaniah now looks to a time after the day of the Lord. Judgment has fallen, enemies have been defeated and those that were hidden (2:3) are now free to truly live.

God's people rejoice
Read Zephaniah 3:14-16

There are four different commands for God's people to lift up their voices in verse 14: sing aloud, shout, rejoice and be glad.

> ❷ *On which occasions do people usually break out into singing?*
> ❷ *What four reasons are given for them, and us, to celebrate like this (v 15)?*

The Lord has taken away their judgments (forgiveness), the Lord has cleared away enemies (victory), the Lord is in their midst (presence) and they shall never fear again (safety). This is celebrating God's full and final victory over all his enemies, all sin and even death itself.

···· TIME OUT ····

Read Revelation 21:1-4

> ❷ *How are these two passages similar?*

In this passage in Zephaniah the people are not the only ones rejoicing...

God rejoices
Read Zephaniah 3:17

God is now free to dwell among his people: it is the culmination of the storyline that has run from creation (Genesis 3:8) right through to new creation (Revelation 21:3). As God looks out across his gathered remnant people he is delighted, he is tender and he rejoices alongside his people in the completed kingdom work they will now experience for ever.

This is the only place in Scripture where God is said to sing and rejoice. We get a glimpse in Luke 15 where there is celebration over lost things being found. But here God rejoices over all the lost people in the world that have been found and brought home.

> ❷ *How does Zephaniah 3:17 make you feel?*

God gathers his people
Read Zephaniah 3:18-20

This new civilisation is unlike the previous regime. Far from being run by ravenous wolves and roaring lions, God will be caring towards the mourning, the lame, the outcasts and when he does, all their shame will be transformed into praise.

> ❷ *What are some of the big lessons you have learnt from the book of Zephaniah?*
> ❷ *What one thing would you like to do as a result of God's word to you, spoken through this much overlook prophet?*

ECCLESIASTES: Pointless?

How do we make sense of life in a broken world? The writer of Ecclesiastes will give us some thought-provoking answers.

....

Read Ecclesiastes 1:1-3

❓ *What do we learn about the writer in verse 1?*

❓ *How would you describe his opening statement in verses 2-3?*

❓ *In what ways is it surprising that such verses are in the Bible?*

Reading Ecclesiastes is a bracing experience! There is no other book in the Bible like it. The writer is very realistic about the troubles of life, and wants us to be honest about those difficulties.

He calls himself "the Teacher" in verse 1, and mentions he was the "son of David, king of Jerusalem". This sounds like Solomon, but he never tells us. We'll simply call him "the teacher".

The word "meaningless" comes 35 times in the book. It means something like "breath" or "mist"—think of your breath on a cold winter's day—here for a moment, then gone! Life, the teacher will tell us, is like that—fleeting, like a breath. So can we really make sense of it all?

Another phrase he constantly uses is "under the sun", verse 3. We'll see that this simply refers to real life in our broken, messed-up world. Life often doesn't make sense, and this is true both for believers and unbelievers. The teacher will help us make sense of it, while never claiming to give us all the answers. Remember too that Ecclesiastes is a part of the Bible called

wisdom literature. Books like Proverbs, Job, Song of Songs and Ecclesiastes are there to help us live wisely in the world God has made, but a world wrecked by human sin.

Face up to reality

Read Ecclesiastes 1:4-11

❓ *What do you think is the main point the writer is wanting to show us?*

❓ *In what ways do these verses match your own experience of life?*

- *For example, verse 9, "There is nothing new under the sun".*
- *Or verse 11, "no one remembers the former generations".*

❓ *How might such realism about life be helpful for us?*

Reading Ecclesiastes might feel a bit gloomy sometimes. But there will be much encouragement along the way! And the teacher will help us to have godly expectations for our lives.

⌃ Pray

Talk to God about your feelings of living in a broken world. Pray he'd teach you wonderful things through Ecclesiastes.

Looking for answers

Is it possible to find meaning in a broken world? The teacher is going to try very hard! And he starts his quest by investigating several different things this world has to offer.

First on the list is something close to all our hearts: *education*. Get the best qualification possible; go to the best college; get the best possible teachers! *But what does it all achieve?*

Worthless degrees

Read Ecclesiastes 1:12-18

❷ *What does the teacher discover from his investigations?*

❷ *What do you think he means in verse 15?*

❷ *How can more knowledge lead to more grief (v 18)?*

The teacher gives himself to study and investigation: "All that is done under the heavens" (v 13). As "king over Israel", (v 12), he clearly has access to the finest teachers and facilities. But his conclusion is that it's all a "chasing after the wind". For all his study, it doesn't help him to find real meaning. Pursuit of knowledge in itself can never satisfy, because you can never know everything! And the more you know, the more you realise you don't know! Simply gaining more understanding of the world around us and about human culture might be fun and enjoyable, but it doesn't make you truly "wise" before God. True wisdom is found elsewhere (see Proverbs 1:7).

Worthless wealth

Read Ecclesiastes 2:1-11

The teacher moves to the next few items on his bucket list. Will these provide the meaning he craves?

❷ *What does the teacher now investigate?*

❷ *What is his conclusion?*

As king over Israel, the teacher has the resources to fulfil his quest for pleasure. He does it all, so we don't need to! Culture, building projects, vast wealth, sex. Although, notice in verses 3 and 9 he says he keeps his wisdom with him—he still wants to think about it all! But in the end, none of it truly satisfies!

⌄ Apply

The teacher's investigations are a challenge to a world which seeks academic achievement and material gain as some of the highest goals we can strive for. We're often told such things will satisfy us and bring us lasting contentment. Jesus himself exposes the futility of such thinking (Matthew 6:19-21), and points the way to real satisfaction.

❷ *How might the teacher's words help you to have a realistic expectation of learning and pleasure?*

❷ *How do his words warn you against investing too heavily in these things?*

❷ *How do Jesus' words in Matthew 6 show us what real satisfaction looks like?*

Light in the darkness

Life in a broken world can be frustrating and hard. And although life as a believer in Jesus offers joy and peace—it can often feel very different in daily life.

Ecclesiastes helps us to understand what life in a broken world is like. We live in a world that experiences the effects of the fall, described in Genesis 3. The teacher is helping us to see that truth. He's giving us permission to feel sad and frustrated by life in a world after Genesis 3; that it's a normal Christian experience, and shouldn't surprise us. And whilst his lessons can sometimes be very blunt—goads, as he calls them in Ecclesiastes 12:11—there are shafts of light that shine throughout the book. Today, we come across one of those shafts. *But first....*

A painful lesson

Read Ecclesiastes 2:12-16

❷ *What is the teacher's discovery here?*
❷ *How does death put all our achievements into perspective?*

⌄ Apply

One of the helpful perspectives that the teacher gives us in Ecclesiastes is the understanding that we are mortal. Death is the great leveller. No matter what our earthly achievements, we must all face death one day. And knowing this enables us to live wisely today.

❷ *It might feel morbid to think about, but why is it really important for us to have this perspective? (For some help, see Psalm 90:9-12).*

Heigh-ho, Heigh-ho...

Read Ecclesiastes 2:17-23

❷ *What does the teacher discover about work?*

This isn't the only thing the Bible says about work! But it's a reminder that work in a world after Genesis 3 can be frustrating and hard. See Genesis 3:17-19! *But...*

A ray of hope?

Read Ecclesiastes 2:24-26

❷ *What does the writer say we need to do?*
❷ *How does this put our frustration and pain into perspective?*

Life in God's world is a gift, not something to be gained. The teacher will show us how we need to embrace the Giver, and then we'll be able to enjoy his gifts, even if we do experience many dark days in our lives! The light of knowing God will enable us to cope with the darkness of living in a broken world.

⌃ Pray

Ask God to help you have a godly perspective on your life and your death, and to be thankful for the gifts he gives you each day. Name some of those gifts before him now.

Making sense of time

Time shapes everything we do. Just count the number of clocks in your house! The teacher will give us a deeper perspective on the how we think about time.

Ecclesiastes 3 is probably the most well-known part of the book. The poem in verses 1-8 is often said in school assemblies and funerals, and was even used as the lyrics of a chart-topping song in the 1960s. But why did the teacher pen this poem, and what does he want us to understand from it?

Round and round we go

Read Ecclesiastes 3:1-8

❷ *In what ways are these verses a summary of human life?*

❷ *What do you think the writer is wanting us to see through the way he structures the poem? For example, the opposite experiences in each verse.*

❷ *How does the poem make you feel about life?*

The poem begins in verse 2 with birth and death, and then contains everything in the middle! It's as if the teacher is describing in poetic form all the different experiences of human life thrown together—perhaps because that is how we experience things. It's worth noting too how many of these experiences we can control. Many of them are reactions to events *out* of our control. But all the while, time ticks on endlessly between our birth to our death. The teacher wants us to see that human life is lived between those two realities, and in between we can do very little to control things!

Making sense of it?

Read Ecclesiastes 3:9-15

❷ *What does the writer say God has "set" in human hearts?*

❷ *What do you think he means by this?*

❷ *How might this change the way we view our time between birth and death?*

❷ *What is his conclusion in verses 12-13?*

Every so often, the teacher shows us some light. These verses are a bit of light in the darkness of living in a broken world. Human beings are made for relationship with God—he's set eternity in our hearts. We're meant to enjoy the gifts he gives us. Our limited time on earth focuses our hearts on enjoying him and making the most of the gifts he gives us.

Apply

❷ *How does having this perspective on our time change the way we view our lives?*

❷ *How can it stop us from despair and lead us to contentment in God?*

Pray

Work through the poem in verses 1-8 and pray for the people who are going through the things it describes. Ask that God would make himself known to them in and through those experiences.

Introduce a friend to

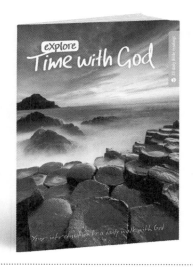

explore

If you're enjoying using *Explore*, why not introduce a friend? *Time with God* is our introduction to daily Bible reading and is a great way to get started with a regular time with God. It includes 28 daily readings along with articles, advice and practical tips on how to apply what the passage teaches.

Why not order a copy for someone you would like to encourage?

Coming up next…

- Ecclesiastes
  with Nathan Buttery

- 1 Corinthians
  with Andrew Wilson & Katy Morgan

- Isaiah
  with Tim Chester & Katy Morgan

- Deuteronomy
  with Frank Price

- Psalms
  with Tim Thornborough

- Christmas from Luke's Gospel

Mere Evangelism
10 Insights From C.S. Lewis to Help You Share Your Faith

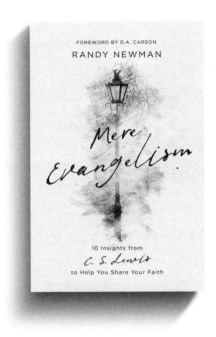

Randy Newman skillfully helps us to draw inspiration and practical help from C.S. Lewis in our evangelism. Each chapter focuses on one of the methods C.S. Lewis used—storytelling, humour, imagery and more—so that we can shape our own conversations, talk about our faith and engage with unbelievers wisely and winsomely. A superb and revealing book that will help you share Jesus with others.

thegoodbook.co.uk/mere-evangelism
thegoodbook.com/mere-evangelism